William H. Helfand, Tilden & Co.

Formulae for making Tinctures, Infusions, Syrups, Wines, Mixtures, Pills

simple and compound, from the fluid & solid extracts

William H. Helfand, Tilden & Co.

Formulae for making Tinctures, Infusions, Syrups, Wines, Mixtures, Pills
simple and compound, from the fluid & solid extracts

ISBN/EAN: 9783337291372

Printed in Europe, USA, Canada, Australia, Japan

Cover: Foto ©Andreas Hilbeck / pixelio.de

More available books at **www.hansebooks.com**

FORMULÆ

FOR MAKING

TINCTURES, INFUSIONS, SYRUPS, WINES,
MIXTURES, PILLS, &c.,

SIMPLE AND COMPOUND,

FROM THE

FLUID & SOLID EXTRACTS,

PREPARED AT THE

LABORATORY OF TILDEN & CO.,

NEW LEBANON, N.Y.

ESTABLISHED IN 1848.

TILDEN & COMPANY,
NEW LEBANON, N. Y.,
AND
98 JOHN STREET, NEW YORK CITY.

1861.

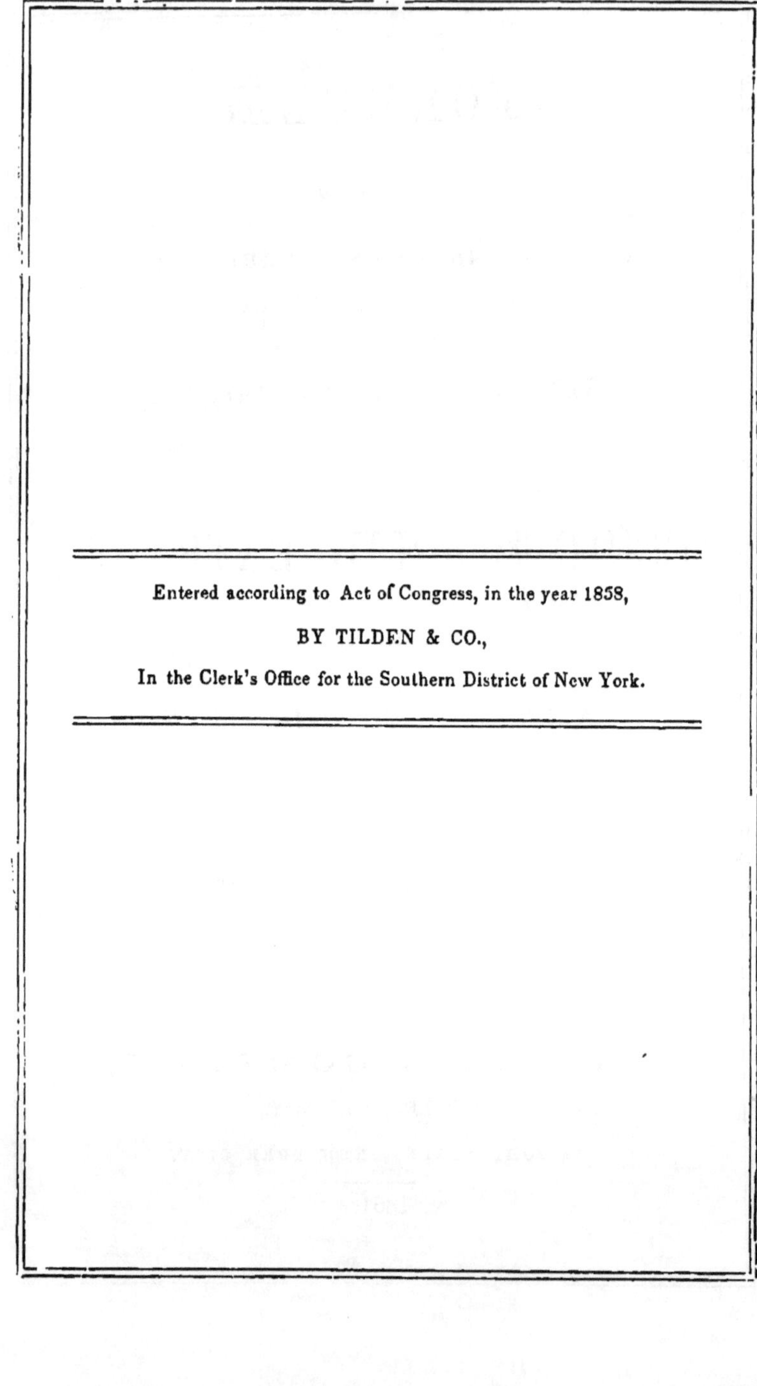

PREFACE.

The numerous inquiries made by those who are engaged in the sale and use of our Fluid Extracts in regard to the proper mode of preparing from them tinctures, infusions, syrups and the like, so as to conform to the officinal strength, suggested the idea of publishing, for the use of such, a series of Formulæ which should embrace selections of the more common and valuable preparations of vegetable agents, as contained in the Pharmacopeias, Dispensatories, Formularies, and other pharmaceutic publications, carefully adapted to the use of our Fluid Extracts. This rendering of established Formulæ could not be given accurately by those who were ignorant of the exact relation the Extracts bear to the crude materials, whence they are derived; and while this relation is intended, in most instances, to be uniform, that is, dram for dram, still, from a variety of circumstances, in many cases, there is a variation to the one side or the other of this line.

It was a matter of early suggestion, that an immense amount of labor could be saved in making these preparations by the use of Fluid Extracts, and, at the same time, a greater degree of accuracy be insured; for the common modes demand more or less extensive apparatus, as well as involve much delay, and a degree of uncertainty attaches to the efficiency of the menstruum employed, unless greater care is given, than usually happens, when prepared in small quantities, and to meet the demands of a limited trade. However, in the case of the Fluid Extracts, the pharmaceutic labor has been expended, with every possible facility for the complete exhaustion of the active properties, and the preparation, in a limited and definite form, is ready for composition and mixture, and the ease and readiness with which these combinations can be made, a slight examination of the following pages will suffice to show.

The object of this Book, then, is to give the requisite data for putting up officinal formulæ, by the use of our Fluid and Solid Extracts. It contains :

1st.—A list of our various preparations of vegetable medicinal agents, including Fluid and Solid Extracts, Resinoids, Alkaloids, Sugar-Coated Pills and Granules.

2nd.—An adaptation of the various simple preparations of the Pharmacopeias, such as tinctures, infusions, syrups and wines.

3rd.—An adaptation of numerous choice and valuable compound Formulæ, selected from reliable, standard authorities.

This *adaptation*, as we have chosen to term it, is such a statement of the original Formulæ, both as respects proportionate strength of mixture and correspondence of doses, as shall require no change in their administration in professional practice, and no further modification for their incorporation into other compound Formulæ. By this method, in the preparation of the simple Formulæ, no manipulations are needed, beyond the complete admixture of the parts, thus reducing to its minimum the labor of preparing them for immediate or future use, requiring for other quantities than those laid down in the text, no other precaution than accuracy in proportioning the components of the Formula.

The directions of the United States Dispensatory (eleventh edition, 1858), for the administration of the crude materials, have been taken as the basis for the calculation of doses; and in the cases of medicines, non-officinal, that is, those not recognized in the United States and British Pharmacopeias, those authorities have been taken as standard which seemed most reliable. The most diligent and careful examination of a large number of authorities at our disposal, has been instituted, in every instance where disagreement or doubt existed, and every point, whether of greater or less importance, has been thoroughly investigated, revised and compared, in the endeavor to secure, if possible, the utmost accuracy. In a number of instances the minimum and maximum doses are widely separated, particularly those of the more powerful and active medicines, so as to give the practitioner the largest liberty in the exercise of his judgment in administering them. It may safely be assumed, in every case, that the error is on the side of the lesser quantity, the doses being made small to avoid mistake.

In the Formulæ contained in the following pages, there is a strict adherence to a uniform system of weights and measurement. The Imperial measures of the British, and the Decimal system of the French Pharmacopeias, have been made to conform to the system in use in this country, to avoid confusion, and facilitate the preparation of prescriptions. A few facts, however, need to be noted.

No specific mention has been made of drams and ounces, whether by measurement or weight, but in all cases LIQUIDS are reckoned by FLUID OUNCES AND DRAMS, while SOLIDS are to be taken by WEIGHT.

With a view to convenience, the DROPS have been estimated from the bottle, and not from the minim glass; and in the following Formulæ, an allowance, justified by actual and repeated experiment, has been made in every case where it was called for, proportioned to the density of the Extract, as well as for the variation from the minim measure. Drops of different fluids, or of the same fluids, under different circumstances, are not equivalent to minims, noi do they sustain to them similar and exact proportions. The extent to which measurement by drops and minims occur in general Formulæ rendered this an important point in our adaptation, and many cases where the doses appear too large, may be accounted for by the smallness of the drops.

In a large number of cases in the formation of Tinctures, 12 and 14 ounces of diluted alcohol are made use of instead of the Pint, as given in the original Formulæ. The object of this change has sometimes been to regulate the dose more accurately, with a diminution of bulk, and again, to facilitate the subdivisions of the proportionate quantities of the compounds, when a less amount was desired.

The Diluted Alcohol made use of in the formation of Tinctures must be prepared with especial care to prevent them from being turbid and opaque. It is requisite that the Diluted Alcohol contain *equal parts* of alcohol and water; but if the officinal directions be followed, this proportion will not be arrived at, for commercial alcohol contains only 85 per cent. of absolute alcohol, thus making, if an equal amount of water be added, 115 parts of water to 85 parts of alcohol in the dilution. The true proportion would be 70 parts of water to the 100 parts of commercial alcohol, or, what is the same, to every 10 *parts of alcohol of* 85 *per cent. add* 7 *parts of water.* Sometimes, when several extracts are united in a compound preparation, the mixture will be slightly turbid, owing to the varying quantities of resinous matter in each; this, however, will be remedied by the addition of a small quantity of pure alcohol. The following table, taken from the U. S. Dispensatory, shows the specific gravity of different mixtures by weight of absolute alcohol and distilled water, at the temperature of 60°. In the notes are placed, referring to their respective specific gravities in the table, the names of the different officinal spirits, whereby the per centage of absolute alcohol is indicated, which they severally contain.

100 Parts.		Sp. Gr. at 60°.	100 Parts		Sp. Gr. at 60°.	100 Parts		Sp. Gr. at 60°.	100 Parts		Sp. Gr. at 60°.
Alc.	Wat		Alc.	Wat		Alc.	Wat		Alc.	Wat	
100	0	.796a	76	24	.857	52	48	.912p	28	72	.962
99	1	.798	75	25	.860	51	49	.915	27	73	.963
98	2	.801	74	26	.863	50	50	.917	26	74	.965
97	3	.804	73	27	.865	49	51	.920q	25	75	.967
96	4	.807	72	28	.867	48	52	.922	24	76	.968
95	5	.809	71	29	.870	47	63	.924	23	77	.970
94	6	.812	70	30	.871	46	54	.926	22	78	.972
93	7	.815	69	31	.874	45	55	.928	21	79	.973
92	8	.817d	68	32	.875	44	56	.930	20	80	.974
91	9	.820	67	33	.879	43	57	.933	19	81	.975
90	10	.822	66	34	.880	42	58	.935u	18	82	.977
89	11	.825g	65	35	.883	41	59	.937	17	83	.978
88	12	.827	64	36	.886	40	60	.939	16	84	.979
87	13	.830	63	37	.889	39	61	.941	15	85	.981
86	14	.832	62	38	.891	38	62	.943	14	86	.982
85	15	.835h	61	39	.893	37	63	.945	13	87	.984
84	16	.838k	60	40	.896	36	64	.947	12	88	.986
83	17	.840n	59	41	.898	35	65	.949	11	89	.987
82	18	43	58	42	.900	34	66	.951	10	90	.988
81	19	.846	57	43	.903	33	67	.953	9	91	.989
80	20	.848	56	44	.904	32	68	.955	8	92	.990
79	21	.851	55	45	.906	31	69	.957	7	93	.991
78	22	.853	54	46	.908	30	70	.958	6	94	.992
77	23	.855	53	47	.910	29	71	.960			

a Alcohol, *Ed.*, *Dub.* *d* Spiritus Fortior, *Dub.* (nearly).
g Lightest spirit obtained by ordinary distillation *h* Alcohol, *U. S.*
k Spiritus Rectificatus, *Lond.*, *Ed.* *n* Spiritus Rectificatus, *Dub.*
p Spiritus Tennior, *Ed.* *q* Spiritus Tenuior, *Lond.*, *Dub.*
u Alcohol Dilutum, *U. S.*

No decoctions have been given, inasmuch as no other process, than mere mixture with water, is needed to afford a full suspension of the active agent in that liquid; so that the extract can be diluted to any extent deemed necessary by the prescriber, although definite Formulæ for their preparation have been given.

These infusions should not be made with hot or boiling water, if they are to stand for any length of time; in that, if exposed, the alcoholic menstruum will evaporate, and the agent itself be precipitated.

A number of infusions and tinctures, seldom, if ever used alone, have been added, that they may easily be prepared if needed for compounds.

Syrups, needed for compounds, may be prepared by substituting *simple syrup* for the water of infusions.

Pills may readily be prepared from the Solid Extracts by taking for each pill a quantity intermediate between the minimum and maximum doses. So, for compound pills, the medium dose of each of the Solid Extracts required should be taken, and afterwards moulded together into pills; the size of which will depend upon the number of components, while the number for a dose must be ascertained by reference to the doses given for the Solid Extracts.

The United States Pharmacopeia five-grain pills, made and sugar-coated at our establishment, are often reduced to the size of three grains, the coating making them too large for convenience. Most of the larger pills, instead of being globular, are made long and conical at each end, to render them more easy of deglutition. Some of the more common medicines are put up both in quarter, half, and also one-grain pills, that several kinds may be taken in combination, the dose of each remaining small.

All the pills referred to in each section, under the head of "Preparations," throughout this book, are prepared and sugar-coated by us.

The Formulæ contained in this book will suggest to apothecaries the mode of preparing others by the aid of the Fluid and Solid Extracts.

The botanical names are, in the main, those furnished by the United States Dispensatory of Wood & Bache; preference has sometimes been given to the arrangement of King's American Eclectic Dispensatory, and, as in this, they follow the catalogic order of their respective genera.

The principal sources whence these Formulæ have been taken are the *U. S. Dispensatory of Wood & Bache*, *King's American Eclectic Dispensatory*, *Pareira's Materia Medica*, *Christison's and Griffith's Dispensatory*, *Royle's Materia Medica*, *Griffith's Formulary*, *Ellis' Medical Formulary*, *Parrish's Practical Pharmacy*, *Tully's Materia Medica*, *Redwood's Supplement to the Pharmacopeia*, *Foote's Practitioner's Pharmacopeia*, *Materia Medica of Edwards and Vavasseur*, *Reese's Formulary*, *Traite de l'art de formuler par Trousseau & Reveil*, *Bouchardat's Manuel de Mateire Medicale, de Therapeutique et de Pharmacie*; also, much valuable matter has been appropriated from files of the following journals: *London Chemical Gazette*, *London Pharmaceutical Journal*, *American Journal of Pharmacy*, *New York Journal of Pharmacy*, *Braithwaite's Retrospect*, *New York Journal of Medicine*, *American Journal of Medical Sciences*, *American Medical Monthly*, *College Journal*, *New Jersey Medical Reporter*, *American Medical Gazette*, *New York Medical Times*, *North Western Medical and Surgical Journal*, *Boston Medical and Surgical Journal*, *Western Lancet*, *New Orleans Medical and Surgical Journal*, *Cincinnati Eclectic Medical Journal*, *Memphis Medical Recorder*, *Virginia Medical Journal*, *New York Register of Medicine and Pharmacy*, *Charleston Medical Journal and Review*, *Ohio Medical and Surgical Journal*, *Iowa Medical Journal*, *Middle States Medical Reformer*, *Rochester Eclectic Journal*, &c., &c.

Wherever private formulæ have been used, and the instances are numerous, it has been the intention to give credit for them; still, by some inadvertence, this may not, in every case, have been done.

The Miscellaneous Department contains a great variety of Formulæ, in some of which no change has been made, but which were inserted in consideration of the especial beauty and specific application. Wherever substitution has been made, the greatest care has been taken to preserve the shape and force of the original.

Immediately preceding the Formulæ is a list of articles prepared in their various forms at our establishment, in *New Lebanon*, *New York*, the most of which are referred to in this work. The utmost care, united with the latest scientific developments in the adaptation of improved apparatus, is expended to make these preparations uniform and reliable. The Solid Extracts have, to a great extent, superseded those formerly imported in large quantities from England and Germany, which, with the Fluid Extracts, introduced at the first by us to the notice of the Profession, are extensively in use throughout the United States and Canadas, and this, too, with the most satisfactory results, for which we need no other or better proof than the continually increasing demand upon us for these preparations.

In our Laboratory are eleven evaporating pans, from which the air is exhausted by a powerful air-pump, and in the vacuum thus formed the evaporation is carried on at a low temperature, while in connection with, and contiguous to our establishment, is a garden of some forty acres, under rich cultivation, by the products of which a demand is met, which, if we were wholly dependent upon the markets for material, it would be impossible for us to do.

The strictest attention is given to accuracy in mixing and proportioning the materials for the Pills, the efficiency of which is testified to be in nowise diminished, while their agreeableness is immeasurably enhanced by their being sugar-coated before being sent into the market. The Alkaloid and Resinoid Department is under the charge of an experienced chemist, whose efforts are wholly confined to the resolution of these concentrated preparations in a form free from all admixture or impurities. New preparations are added to our list as occasion seems to demand, it being the intention to give a full supply of all those articles that come legitimately within the range of our business.

This publication of Formulæ we shall continue in each succeeding issue of our JOURNAL OF MATERIA MEDICA AND PHARMACEUTIC FORMULARY, in such a form that they can be cut out and preserved with the others in this book. We trust that these Formulæ will prove a satisfactory reply to those whose repeated inquiries incited to their publication.

TILDEN & CO.

NEW LEBANON, N. Y., May, 1858.

LIST OF

SOLID AND FLUID EXTRACTS,

ALKALOIDS AND RESINOIDS,

PHARMACEUTIC SUGAR-COATED PILLS AND GRANULES,

With the minimum and maximum doses.

SOLID EXTRACTS.

	Articles.	Doses.	
Solid Ext.	Aconitum	¼ to 1	Grain.
"	Anthemis, (*Chamomile,*)	4 to 20	"
"	Artemisia, (*Wormwood,*)	3 to 5	"
"	Asclepias Inc. (*White Indian Hemp,*)	3 to 5	"
"	Apocynum Andros. (*Bitter-root,*)	2 to 8	"
"	" Cannab. (*Indian Hemp,*)	1 to 5	"
"	Belladonna	¼ to 1	"
"	Cannabis Ind. (*Ind. Hemp, Foreign,*)	1 to 2	"
"	Chimaphila, (*Prince's Pine,*)	10 to 20	"
"	Chelidonium, (*Celandine,*)	5 to 10	"
"	Cimicifuga, (*Black Cohosh,*)	4 to 8	"
"	Colocynthis, (*Colocynth.*) Used in Compounds.		
"	" Compositum	2 to 30	"
"	Colombo	4 to 10	"
"	Conium	½ to 1½	"
"	Cornus Florida, (*Boxwood,*)	5 to 10	"
"	Cubeba	2 to 20	"
"	Cypripedium, (*Ladies' Slipper,*)	5 to 15	"
"	Digitalis, (*Foxglove,*)	½ to 1	"
"	Dulcamara, (*Bittersweet,*)	3 to 8	"
"	Eupatorium, (*Boneset,*)	5 to 20	"
"	Filix Mas, (*Male Fern,*)	9 to 15	"
"	Gentiana	3 to 15	"
"	Geranium Mac. (*Cranesbill,*)	3 to 15	"
"	Hæmatoxylon, (*Logwood,*)	5 to 30	"
"	Helleborus, (*Black Hellebore,*)	1 to 5	"
"	Humulus, (*Hop,*)	5 to 20	"
"	Hydrastis, (*Golden Seal.*)	2 to 5	"
"	Hyoscyamus, (*Henbane,*)	½ to 1	"
"	Ignatia Amara, (*Ignatia Bean,*)	½ to 1½	"

Solid Ext.	Iris Versicol, (*Blue Flag,*)	1 to 4	Grains.
"	Jalapa	3 to 8	"
"	Juglans, (*Butternut,*)	5 to 20	"
"	Krameria, (*Rhatany,*)	5 to 20	"
"	Lactuca, (*Lettuce,*)	2 to 5	"
"	Lappa, (*Burdock,*)	5 to 20	"
"	Leontice Thalic. (*Blue Cohosh,*)	1 to 5	"
"	Leonurus, (*Motherwort,*)	3 to 6	"
"	Marrubium, (*Horehound,*)	5 to 10	"
"	Nux Vomica	½ to 1	"
"	Papaver, (*Poppy,*)	3 to 10	"
"	Phytolacca, (*Poke,*)	1 to 4	"
"	Podophyllum, (*Mandrake,*)	3 to 12	"
"	Polygonum, (*Water Pepper,*)	2 to 3	"
"	Quassia	3 to 5	"
"	Quercus Alba, (*White Oak,*)	10 to 20	"
"	Rheum, (*Rhubarb,*)	2 to 10	"
"	Rumex Crispa, (*Yellow Dock,*)	4 to 8	"
"	Rubus Villosus, (*Blackberry,*)	4 to 6	"
"	Ruta, (*Rue,*)	2 to 4	"
"	Sabina, (*Savin,*)	1 to 5	"
"	Sanguinaria, (*Bloodroot,*)	½ to 5	"
"	Sarsaparilla, Amer	5 to 20	"
"	" " Compd	5 to 20	"
"	" Rio Negro	5 to 15	"
"	" " Compd	5 to 15	"
"	Senna Alex	3 to 8	"
"	Spiræa, (*Hardhack,*)	2 to 5	"
"	Stramonium	½ to 1	"
"	Taraxacum, (*Dandelion,*)	10 to 20	"
"	Trifolium, (*Red Clover.*) Used externally.		
"	Uva Ursi	5 to 15	"
"	Valerian, (English,)	3 to 10	"
"	Veratrum Viride, (*White Hellebore,*)	⅓ to ½	"

ALKALOIDS AND RESINOIDS.

Articles.	Doses.	
Aletrin, (*Star Grass,*)	1 to 3	Grains.
Alnuin, (*Tag Alder,*)	1 to 3	"
Apocynin, (*Bitter Root,*)	½ to 2	"
Asclepidin, (*Pleurisy Root,*)	1 to 5	"
Baptisin, (*Wild Indigo,*)	¼ to ½	"
Caulophylin, (*Blue Cohosh,*)	¼ to 4	"

Chelonin, (*Balmony.*)	1	to	2	Grains.
Cimicifugin, (*Macrotin,*)	1	to	6	"
Cornin, (*Boxwood.*)	1	to	10	"
Corydalin, (*Turkey Corn,*)	½	to	1	"
Cypripedin	2	to	4	"
Dioscorein, (*Wild Yam,*)	1	to	6	"
Eupatorin, (*Boneset,*)	1	to	2	"
Eupurpurin, (*Queen of the Meadow,*)	3	to	4	"
Gelseminin, (*Yellow Jessamine,*)	½	to	2	"
Geraniin, (*Cranesbill,*)	1	to	5	"
Helonin, (*Unicorn,*)	½	to	1	"
Hydrastin, (Resinoid,)	½	to	5	"
Hydrastin, (Neutral,)	2	to	6	"
Hydrastina, (Alkaloid,)	1	to	5	"
Hyoscyamin, (*Henbane,*)	⅛	to	½	"
Iridin, (*Blue Flag,*)	½	to	5	"
Jalapin, (*Jalap,*)	1	to	2	"
Juglandin, (*Butternut,*)	1	to	5	"
Leptandrin, (*Culver's Root,*)	½	to	2	"
Liatrin, (*Button Snake Root,*)	4	to	8	"
Lobelin, (*Lobelia,*)	½	to	1½	"
Lupulin, (*Hop.*)	6	to	10	"
Myricin, (*Bayberry,*)	2	to	10	"
Phytolaccin, (*Garget or Poke,*)	¼	to	1	"
Podophyllin, (*Mandrake,*)	⅛	to	3	"
Populin, (*Poplar,*)	4	to	8	"
Prunin, (*Cherry bark,*)	2	to	6	"
Rhusin, (*Sumach,*)	1	to	2	"
Rumin, (*Yellow Dock,*)	4	to	8	"
Salicin, (*Willow,*)	2	to	10	"
Sanguinarin, Resinoid, (*Blood Root,*)	½	to	2	"
Sanguinarina, Alkaloid, "	$\frac{1}{30}$	to	$\frac{1}{10}$	"
Scutellarin, (*Scullcap,*)	2	to	6	"
Senecin, (*Life Root,*)	3	to	5	"
Stillingin, (*Queens' Delight,*)	2	to	5	"
Trilliin, (*Beth Root,*)	4	to	8	"
Veratrin, (*Hellebore,*)	$\frac{1}{10}$	to	½	"
Xanthoxylin, (*Prickly Ash,*)	2	to	6	"

FLUID EXTRACTS.

Articles.	Doses.
Fluid Ext. Aconite	2 to 8 Drops.
" Aletris	10 to 30 "
" Arbutus, (*Epigæa*,)	1 to 2 Drams.
" Arnica	10 to 60 Drops.
" Balmony, (*Chelone*,)	1 to 2 Drams.
" Bayberry, (*Myrica*,)	1 to 2 "
" Belladonna	3 to 10 Drops.
" Bethroot	1 to 3 Drams.
" Bitter-root, (*Apocy. Andros.*)	10 Drops to 1 Dram.
" Bittersweet, (*Dulcamara*,)	½ to 1 "
" Black Alder, (*Prinos*,)	1 to 2 Drams.
" Blackberry, (*Rubus Villosus*,)	½ to 1 Dram.
" Black Cohosh, (*Cimicifuga*,)	½ to 2 "
" " " Comp.	½ to 1 "
" Black Hellebore	10 to 20 Drops.
" Black Pepper	10 to 40 "
" Bloodroot, (*Sanguinaria*,)	5 to 60 "
" Blue Cohosh, (*Leontice*,)	15 to 40 "
" Blue Flag, (*Iris*,)	20 to 60 "
" Boneset, (*Eupatorium Perfo.*)	1 to 2 Drams.
" Boxwood, (*Cornus Florida*,)	½ to 2 "
" Buchu, (*Barosma*,)	½ to 2 "
" " Comp'd,	½ to 2 "
" Buckthorn, (*Rhamnus*,)	1 to 1½ "
" Bugle, (*Lycopus*,)	1 to 2 "
" Burdock, (*Lappa*,)	1 to 2 "
" Butternut, (*Juglans*,)	1 to 2 "
" Canella	15 to 30 Drops.
" Capsicum,	5 to 15 "
" Catnip, (*Nepeta*,)	2 to 4 Drams.
" Cascarilla	20 to 30 Drops.
" Celandine, Great	10 to 20 "
" Chamomile, (*Anthemis*,)	½ to 1 Dram.
" Cherry Bark	2 to 4 "
" " " Comp'd	½ to 2 "
" Cinchona	½ to 1 "
" " Comp'd. (U. S. P.)	½ to 1 "
" " Red	½ to 1 "
" " Calisaya	½ to 1 "
" Colchicum Root	3 to 12 Drops.
" " Seed	5 to 15 "

Fluid Ext.	Colombo	20 to 60 Drops.
"	Conium	5 to 20 "
"	Cotton Root	4 Drams.
"	Craneshill, (*Geranium*,)	½ to 1 "
"	Cubebs	½ to 1½ "
"	" Etherial	1 to 2 "
"	Culver's Root, (*Leptandra*,)	⅓ to 1 "
"	Dandelion, (*Taraxacum*,)	1 to 2 "
"	" Comp'd	1 to 2 "
"	" and Senna	1 to 2 "
"	Ergot, Etherial	½ to 1 "
"	Foxglove, (*Digitalis*,)	5 to 10 Drops.
"	Garget or Poke, (*Phytolacca*,)	10 to 30 "
"	Gelseminum	3 to 20 "
"	Gentian	½ to 1 Dram.
"	" Comp'd	½ to 1 "
"	Gillenia	4 to 12 Drops.
"	Ginger	½ to 1½ Drams.
"	Golden Seal, (*Hydrastis*,)	½ to 2 "
"	Hardhack, (*Spiræa*,)	4 to 20 Drops.
"	Hop, (*Humulus*,)	½ to 1 Dram.
"	Horehound, (*Marrubium*,)	½ to 1 "
"	Hydrangea	1 to 2 "
"	Hyoscyamus	10 to 20 Drops.
"	Ignatia Bean, (*Ignatia Amara*,)	5 to 10 "
"	Indian Hemp, (*Apocy. Cannab.*)	5 to 60 "
"	" " F'gn, (*Cannabis Ind.*)	5 to 10 "
"	" " White, (*Asclepias*,)	20 to 40 "
"	Ipecac	5 Drops to 1 Dram.
"	" and Seneka, (*Jackson*,)	½ to 1 "
"	Jalap	¼ to 1 "
"	Ladies' Slipper, (*Cypripedium*,)	½ to 1 "
"	Lettuce, (*Lactuca*,)	½ to 2 "
"	Liatris	1 to 2 "
"	Life Root, (*Senecio*,)	½ to 1 "
"	Liquorice	2 to 4 "
"	Liverwort	2 to 3 "
"	Lobelia	10 Drops to 1 Dram.
"	" Comp'd	10 " to 1 "
"	Logwood, (*Hæmatoxylon*,)	½ to 1 "
"	Mandrake, (*Podophyllum*,)	½ to 1 "
"	" Comp'd	½ to 2 "
"	Matico, (*Piper Angust.*)	½ to 2 "
"	Nux Vomica	5 to 15 Drops.
"	Opium, Aqueous	10 to 60 "

Fluid Ext.	Orange Peel	½ to	2	Drams.
"	Orris Root. Used in Compounds.			
"	Pareira Brava	½ to	1	Dram.
"	Peppermint	1 to	2	Drams.
"	Pink Root, (*Spigelia*,)	½ to	1½	"
"	" " Comp'd	½ to	2	"
"	" " and Senna	½ to	1	"
"	Pleurisy Root, (*Asclepias*,)	½ to	2	"
"	Poppy	½ to	1	"
"	Prickly Ash, (*Xanthoxylum*,)	15 to	45	Drops.
"	Prince's Pine, (*Chimaphila*,)		1	Dram.
"	Quassia	½ to	1	"
"	Rhatany, (*Krameria*,)	½ to	1	"
"	Rhubarb	½ to	1	"
"	" Aromatic	½ to	1	"
"	" and Senna	½ to	1	"
"	Rue	20 to	40	Drops.
"	Saffron	20 to	60	"
"	Sarsaparilla, Rio Negro		1	Dram.
"	" Comp'd, (U. S. P.)		1	"
"	" and Dandelion		1	"
"	Sassafras	1 to	2	"
"	Savin, (*Sabina*,)	10 to	30	Drops.
"	Scullcap, (*Scutellaria*,)	½ to	1	Dram.
"	" Comp'd	½ to	1	"
"	Seneka	20 to	40	Drops.
"	Senna, (U. S. P.)	1 to	2	Drams.
"	" Aqueous	1 to	2	"
"	" and Jalap	½ to	1	"
"	Serpentaria	¼ to	½	"
"	Skunk Cabbage, (*Symplocarpus*,)	20 to	80	Drops.
"	Spearmint, (*Mentha Viridis*,)	1 to	3	Drams.
"	Squill	2 to	24	Drops.
"	" Comp'd	10 to	20	"
"	Stillingia, (*Queen's Root*,)	20 to	40	"
"	" Comp'd	½ to	1	Dram.
"	Stramonium, (*Thorn Apple*,)	5 to	20	Drops.
"	Sumach, (*Rhus Glabrum*,)	1 to	2	Drams.
"	Tag Alder, (*Alnus Rubra*,)	1 to	2	"
"	Turkey Corn, (*Corydalis*,)	10 to	40	Drops.
"	Turmeric, (*Curcuma*,)	2 to	3	Drams.
"	Unicorn	1 to	3	"
"	Uva Ursi	⅓ to	1	"
"	Valerian	½ to	1½	"

Fluid Ext. Veratrum Viride. (*See page 115.*)

"	Wahoo, (*Euonymus*,)	1 to 2 Drams.
"	Water Pepper, (*Polygonum*,)	10 to 60 Drops.
"	White Oak, (*Quercus Alba*,	½ to 1 Dram.
"	Wild Indigo, (*Baptisia*,)	¼ to ½ "
"	Wintergreen, (*Pyrola*,)	1 to 2 "
"	Witch Hazel, (*Hamamelis*,)	1 to 2 "
"	Wormwood, (*Artemisia*,)	⅓ to ⅔ "
"	Yellow Dock, (*Rumex*,)	1 to 2 "

PILLS.

Articles.	No. of Pills for a Dose.
1/32 Grain each.	
Arsenous Acid	1 to 3
Atropia	1 to 2
Digitalin	1 to 2
Strychnia	1 to 2
Veratria	1 to 3
Morphia	1 to 5
1/16 Grain each.	
Codeia	1 to 4
⅛ Grain each.	
Morphia	1 to 2
Iodine	1 to 4
¼ Grain each.	
Ext. Aconitum	1 to 4
" Belladonna	1 to 4
" Conium	2 to 6
" Hyoscyamus	2 to 4
" Ipecac	1 to 3
" Opium	1 to 2
" Veratrum Viride	1 to 2
Kermes	2 to 4
Nitrate of Silver	1 to 2
Proto-Iodide of Mercury	1 to 2
Tartar Emetic	1 to 2
½ Grain each.	
Ammoniated Copper, (U. S. P.)	1 to 6
Ext. Aconitum	1 to 2
" Belladonna	1 to 2
" Cannabis Indica	2 to 4
" Colchicum	1 to 3

Ext. Conium	1 to 3
" Digitalis	1 to 3
" Hyoscyamus	1 to 2
" Ignatia Amara	1 to 3
" Nux Vomica	1 to 2
" Sanguinaria	1 to 5
" Stramonium	1 to 2
" Veratrum Viride	1 to 2
Iridin	1 to 6
Sanguinarin	1 to 4
Santonin	2 to 4
Phytolaccin	1 to 2
Piperin	2 to 4
Podophyllin	2 to 6
Quinia, Valerianate of	1 to 3

1 *Grain each.*

Apocynin	1 to 2
Asclepidin	1 to 5
Capsicum	1 to 2
Cimicifugin	1 to 4
Ext. Aconitum	1 to 2
" Apocynum Cannab	1 to 3
" Belladonna	1 to 2
" Cannabis Ind., (*Ind. Hemp, F'gn,*)	1 to 2
" Conium	1 to 2
" " and Ipecac, (U. S. P.)	3 to 5
" Helleborus, (*Black Hellebore,*)	1 to 5
" Hyoscyamus	1 to 2
" Iris Versicol. (*Blue Flag,*)	1 to 4
" Jalapa	3 to 6
" Krameria, (*Rhatany,*)	2 to 10
" Phytolacca, (*Poke,*)	1 to 4
" Podophyllum, (*Mandrake,*)	3 to 8
" Quassia	3 to 5
" Rheum	2 to 6
" Sabina, (*Savin,*)	1 to 5
" Sanguinaria, (*Blood Root,*)	1 to 5
" Stramonium	1 to 2
Geraniin	1 to 5
Hydrastin, Neutral	2 to 6
Hydrastina, Alkaloid	1 to 5
Iridin	2 to 5
Iron, Lactate of	1 to 2
Iron, Proto-Iodide of	2 to 4

Jalapin	1 to 2
Leptandrin	1 to 2
Opium	1 to 3
Populin	4 to 8
Quevenne's Iron, (*reduced by Hydrogen*,)	3 to 6
Quinia, Sulphate of	1 to 6
Salicin	1 to 5
Sanguinarin	1 to 2
Scutellarin	2 to 6
Stillingin	2 to 5
Tannin	2 to 4
Xanthoxylin	2 to 6

2 *Grains each.*

Anderson's, (*Anti-Bilious and Purgative*,)	1 to 3
Bismuth, Sub-Nitrate of	2 to 4
Calomel	1 to 2
Cornin	1 to 5
Ext. Anthemis, (*Chamomile*,)	2 to 6
" Apocynum Andros. (*Bitter Root*,)	1 to 4
" Asclepias Inc. (*Ind. Hemp, White*,)	2 to 3
" Cimicifuga, (*Black Cohosh*,)	2 to 4
" Colombo	2 to 5
" Cornus Florida, (*Boxwood, Dogwood*,)	2 to 5
" Cubeba	1 to 6
" Cypripedium, (*Ladies' Slipper*,)	2 to 6
" Digitalis and Squill, (U. S. P.)	2 to 4
" Dulcamara, (*Bittersweet*,)	2 to 4
" Eupatorium, (*Boneset*,)	2 to 6
" Filix Mas, (*Male Fern*,)	4 to 7
" Gentiana	2 to 6
" Geranium Mac. (*Cranesbill*,)	2 to 6
" Hæmatoxylon, (*Logwood*,)	2 to 6
" Lactuca, (*Lettuce*,)	1 to 3
" Lappus, (*Burdock*,)	1 to 6
" Leontice Thalictroides, (*Blue Cohosh*,)	1 to 3
" Leonurus, (*Motherwort*,)	1 to 3
" Marrubium, (*Horehound*,)	2 to 5
" Papaver, (*Poppy*,)	2 to 5
" Quercus Alba, (*White Oak*,)	5 to 10
" Rubus Villosus, (*Blackberry*,)	2 to 3
" Rumex Crispa, (*Yellow Dock*,)	1 to 2
" Ruta, (*Rue*,)	1 to 2
" Senna Alex	1 to 2
" Spiræa, (*Hardhack*,)	1 to 4

Ext. Uva Ursi		1 to 7
" Valeriana, (English)		2 to 5
Ipecac and Opium, (*Dover's Powder,*)		2 to 6
Iron, Citrate of		2 to 3
Magnesia, Calcined		2 to 5
" and Rhubarb	1 Grain each.	1 to 4
Opium and Acetate of Lead	1 " "	1 to 3
Potassa, Tartrate of, and Iron		2 to 4
Potassium, Iodide of		1 to 5
Senecin		1 to 3
Sulphur, Washed		2 to 4
Willow Charcoal		2 to 6

$2\frac{1}{2}$ *Grains.*

Blue Pill, (U. S. P.)	$2\frac{1}{2}$ Grains.	2 to 4
" " "	5 "	1 to 3
Hooper's Pills	$2\frac{1}{2}$ "	1 to 3

3 *Grains each.*

Calomel and Opium, (U. S. P.)	1 to 2
Cochia Pill	1 to 3
Colocynth Compound and Blue Pill	2 to 3
" " and Calomel	2 to 3
Compound Calomel, (*Plummer's*)	1 to 2
" Cathartic, improved, (without Calomel)	1 to 3
" " (U. S. P.)	1 to 4
" Iron, (U. S. P.)	2 to 6
Copaiba and Ext. Cubebs	2 to 4
" " " " and Citrate of Iron	1 to 4
Dinner Pill, (*Lady Webster's*)	1 to 3
Ext. Chimaphila, (*Prince's Pine. Pipsissewa.*)	3 to 6
" Colocynth Compound	2 to 6
" " " and Hyoscyamus, (U. S. P.)	1 to 6
" Cubebs and Alum	2 to 4
" " " Ext. Rhatany and Iron	1 to 3
" Rhubarb and Iron, (U. S. P.)	2 to 3
" Sarsaparilla, Amer	2 to 5
" " " Compound	2 to 5
" " Rio Negro	2 to 5
" " " Compound	2 to 5
" Taraxacum, (*Dandelion,*)	3 to 6
Gamboge Compound, (U. S. P.)	3 to 5
Ipecac and Squill, (U. S. P.)	2 to 3
Iron, Carbonate of, (*Vallet's Formula,*)	3 to 10
Manganese, Carbonate of, and Iron	1 to 3

Podophyllin and Blue Pill	1 to 2
Soap and Opium, (U. S. P. Compound.)	1 to 3
Squill Compound, (U. S. P.)	2 to 3
Storax Compound. (U. S. P.)	1 to 4

4 Grains each.

Aloetic, (U. S. P.)	1 to 3
Aloes and Assafœtida, (U. S. P.)	2 to 5
" and Iron, (U. S. P.)	1 to 4
" and Myrrh, (U. S. P.)	3 to 5
" and Ext. Gentian, (U. S. P. Compound.)	1 to 5
Assafœtida, (U. S. P.) without smell.	2 to 4
Cook's Pill	1 to 3
Copaiba, pure solidified	2 to 6
Iron, Sulphate of, (U. S. P.)	1 to 5
Rhubarb and Blue Pill	1 to 2
" Compound, (U. S. P.)	2 to 5
Soda, Bi-Carbonate of	2 to 5

FORMULÆ.

ACONITUM NAPELLUS.

Aconite. Monkshood.

The species recognized by the United States Pharmacopeia, as officinal, is the A. Napellus. The whole plant is possessed of medicinal properties. The leaves and root are generally used separately.

MEDICAL PROPERTIES.

A powerful narcotic. Used in rheumatism, neuralgia, epilepsy, paralysis, amaurosis, scrofula, syphilis, intermittent fever, dropsies, &c. Valuable as an anti-phlogistic remedy, and in cases of active cerebral congestion or inflammation.

PREPARATIONS.

Solid Extract....................................Dose, 1-4 to 1 Grain.
Fluid " .... " 2 to 8 Drops.
Pills..1-4, 1-2, and 1 Grain.

TINCTURE OF ACONITE.

Fluid Extract..............................Two Ounces.
Diluted Alcohol..........................Fourteen Ounces.
Dose—Ten to twenty drops three times a day.

WINE OF ACONITE.

Fluid Extract..........................Two Ounces.
Sherry Wine..............................Fourteen Ounces.
Dose—Ten to twenty drops.

COMPOUND WINE OF ACONITE.

Fluid Extract of Aconite....................One Ounce.
Antimonial Wine..........................Fourteen Ounces.
Dose—Fifteen to twenty drops, till the desired effect is produced.

ACONITE OINTMENT.

Solid Extract of Aconite........................One Part.
Lard ....Two Parts.

ACONITE PLASTER.

Solid Extract of Aconite.

Spread over surface of adhesive plaster. Apply in neuralgic affections to the painful part.

WINE OF ACONITE AND COLCHICUM.

Wine of Aconite.................. ....One Ounce.
Wine of Colchicum Seed.......................Half Ounce.

Dose—Ffteen to twenty drops every three hours.

COMPOUND PILLS OF ACONITE.

Solid Extract of Aconite.......................Half Dram.
Solid Extract of Stramonium..................Four Grains.
Valerianate of Quinia.........................One Scruple.

Mix, and divide into sixty pills.

Dose—One pill every two, three or four hours, according to symptoms. Used in nervous irritability, nervous headache, restlessness and wakefulness

MIXTURE OF ACONITE AND VALERIAN.

Fluid Extract of Aconite.....................Half Dram.
" " Valerian.......................Half Ounce.
Syrup .... .Half Ounce.
Water.... ....Four Ounces.
Liq. Ammonia Acet..........................One Ounce.

Dose—Four drams every two hours.

Used in nervous gout.—*Richter.*

PILLS OF ACONITE AND DOVER'S POWDER.

Solid Extract of Aconite......................Six Grains.
Dover's Powder............................Twelve Grains.
Syrup ....Sufficient.

Make six pills. Take one three times a day in chronic rheumatism. Each pill contains one grain of Aconite and two grains Dover's Powder.

ALETRIS FARINOSA.

Star Grass.

This plant is found in most parts of the United States, usually in dry soils and barrens. The root is the officinal portion.

MEDICAL PROPERTIES.

One of the most intense bitters known. Used in infusion as a tonic and stomachic; large doses produce nausea and a tendency to vomit. Has been employed in chronic rheumatism and dropsy.

PREPARATIONS.

Fluid Extract.................................Dose, 10 to 30 Drops.
Aletridin.................................. " 1 to 3 Grains.

TINCTURE OF ALETRIS.

Fluid Extract.................................Two Ounces.
Diluted Alcohol.................................One Pint.
Dose—Half to one dram.

INFUSION OF ALETRIS.

Fluid Extract.................................Two Drams.
Water.................................One Pint.
Dose—One to two ounces.

SYRUP OF ALETRIS.

Fluid Extract.................................One Ounce.
Syrup.................................One Pint.
Dose—One to two drams.

PILLS OF ALETRIS.

Solid Extract of Aletris.................................Two Grains.
Dioscorein.................................Two "
Ginger.................................Four "
Make two pills. In flatulent colic and borborygmi.

ALNUS RUBRA.

Tag Alder.

A well known shrub, growing in clumps on the borders of ponds and rivers, and in swamps. The bark is the part used in medicine.

MEDICAL PROPERTIES.

Alterative, emetic and astringent. Useful in scrofula, secondary syphilis, and several forms of cutaneous diseases. The *Alnuin* is recommended in herpes, syphilis, scorbutus, impetigo, &c.

PREPARATIONS.

Fluid Extract..Dose, 1 to 2 Drams.
Alnuin .... " 1 to 3 Grains.

INFUSION OF TAG ALDER.

Fluid Extract..Two Ounces.
Water..One Pint.
Dose—One to two ounces.

ANTHEMIS NOBILIS.

Chamomile.

This plant is a native of Europe, where it is largely cultivated for medicinal purposes. The flowers are the part used.

MEDICAL PROPERTIES.

Tonic. Used in cases of enfeebled digestion, general debility and languid appetite. In large doses will act as an emetic.

PREPARATIONS.

Fluid Extract..Dose, 1-2 to 1 Dram.
Solid Extract.. " 4 to 20 Grains.

INFUSION OF CHAMOMILE.

Fluid Extract.............. .... Two Ounces.
Water..One Pint.
Dose—Half to one ounce.

COMPOUND INFUSION OF CHAMOMILE.

Fluid Extract....................................One Ounce.
Essence of Fennel..............................Half Dram.
Water...One Pint.
Dose—One to two ounces.

SYRUP OF CHAMOMILE.

Fluid Extract....................................Four Ounces.
Syrup..Twelve Ounces.
Dose—Two to four drams.

WINE OF CHAMOMILE.

Fluid Extract....................................Two Ounces.
Sherry Wine.....................................One Pint.
Dose—Four to eight drams.

COMPOUND CHAMOMILE PILLS.

Solid Extract of Chamomile..................One Dram.
Solid Extract of Rhubarb.....................Five Grains.
Assafœtida.......................................Half Scruple.
Mix; divide into thirty pills.
Dose—Three times a day in flatulent dyspepsia.

APOCYNUM ANDROSÆMIFOLIUM.

Bitter Root.

An indigenous plant, flowering in June and July. The root is the part employed.

MEDICAL PROPERTIES.

Valuable in the treatment of chronic hepatic affections; used as an emetic and diaphoretic; as an alterative in syphilitic and scrofulous affections, as well as in intermittents and the low stage of typhoid fevers.

PREPARATIONS.

Fluid Extract...........................	Dose,	tonic, 10 to 20 Drops.
" "	"	diaphoretic, 15 to 25 Drops.
" "	"	emetic, 1-2 to 1 Dram.
Solid Extract...........................	"	2 to 8 Grains.
Apocynin	"	1-2 to 2 Grains.
Pills of Apocynin...........................	"	1 Grain each.
Pills of Ext. Apocynum...........................	"	2 Grains each.

TINCTURE OF BITTER ROOT.

Fluid Extract............................Two Ounces.
Diluted Alcohol............................One Pint.

Dose—One to two drams, and half to one ounce.

INFUSION OF BITTER ROOT.

Fluid Extract............................Half Ounce.
Water............................One Pint.

Dose—A wineglassful three times a day.—*Griscom.*

SYRUP OF BITTER ROOT.

Fluid Extract............................One-and-a-half Ounces.
Syrup............................One Pint.

Dose—Two to four drams.

WINE OF BITTER ROOT.

Fluid Extract............................Two Ounces.
Sherry Wine............................One Pint.

Dose—One to two drams.

COMPOUND POWDER OF APOCYNIN.

Apocynin............................Six Grains.
Leptandrin............................ " "
Myricin............................ " "

Dose—One to three grains. Useful in jaundice, as well as in hepatic torpor and constipation.

APOCYNUM CANNABINUM.

Indian Hemp.

An indigenous plant, growing in situations similar to the last. The root is officinal.

MEDICAL PROPERTIES.

Powerfully emetic; in decoction, diuretic and diaphoretic. It produces much nausea, diminishes the frequency of the pulse, and appears to produce drowsiness, independently of the exhaustion consequent upon vomiting. Of magical efficacy in dropsy.

PREPARATIONS.

Fluid Extract.......................... Dose, tonic, 5 to 15 Drops.
" " .... " emetic, 20 to 60 Drops.
Solid Extract.......................... " 1 to 5 Grains.
Pills.................................. " 1 Grain each.

TINCTURE OF INDIAN HEMP.

Fluid Extract............................One Ounce.
Diluted Alcohol..........................One Pint.
Dose—One to two drams, and a half to one ounce.

INFUSION OF INDIAN HEMP.

Fluid Extract............................Half Ounce.
Water....................................One Pint.
Dose—Half to two ounces.

SYRUP OF INDIAN HEMP.

Fluid Extract............................One-and-a-half Ounces
Syrup....................................One Pint.
Dose—Half to one dram.

WINE OF INDIAN HEMP.

Fluid Extract............................Two Drams.
Sherry Wine..............................Eight Ounces.
Dose--One to two drams.

ARCTOSTAPHYLOS UVA URSI.

Uva Ursi.

This is a perennial evergreen, common in the northern part of Europe, Asia and America. The leaves are the medicinal portion.

MEDICAL PROPERTIES.

Uva Ursi is an astringent tonic, and has a specific direction to the urinary organs, for complaints of which it is chiefly used; has reputation as an antilithic in gravel, chronic nephritis, ulceration of the kidneys, bladder and urinary passages. It has been recommended in place of Ergot of Rye. It does not cause such powerful contractions, nor is its use attended with as much danger.

PREPARATIONS.

Fluid Extract..Dose, 1-3 to 1 Dram.
Solid Extract..Dose, 5 to 15 Grains.
Pills.. " 2 Grains each.

TINCTURE OF UVA URSI.

Fluid Extract..Two Ounces.
Diluted Alcohol..One Pint.
Dose—Three to six drams.

INFUSION OF UVA URSI.

Fluid Extract..One Ounce.
Water..One Pint.
Dose—One to two ounees.

SYRUP OF UVA URSI.

Fluid Extract..Eight Ounces.
Syrup..Two Pints.
Dose—Two to four drams.

ARISTOLOCHIA SERPENTARIA.

Virginia Snakeroot.

This plant grows throughout the Middle, Southern and Western States. The root is the officinal part.

MEDICAL PROPERTIES.

A stimulant tonic, used in typhoid fever, whether idiopathic or symptomatic, when the system begins to feel the necessity for support, but is unable to bear active stimulation. Its action may be much improved by combination with Cinchona, particularly in intermittent fevers. Employed as a gargle in malignant sore throat.

PREPARATIONS.

Fluid Extract..Dose, 1-4 to 1-2 Dram.

TINCTURE OF SNAKEROOT.

Fluid Extract..Three Ounces.
Diluted Alcohol..One Pint.
Dose—One to two drams.

INFUSION OF SNAKEROOT.

Fluid Extract............................Half Ounce.
Water.....................................One Pint.

Dose—One to two ounces, in low forms of fever.

SYRUP OF SNAKEROOT.

Fluid Extract............................Two Ounces.
Syrup.....................................One Pint.

Dose—One-and-a-half to three drams.

COMPOUND TINCTURE OF SNAKEROOT.

Fluid Extract of Snakeroot.................Half Ounce.
" " Ipecac.................... " "
" " Saffron.................... " "
" " Ladies' Slipper............. " "
Camphor................................. " "
Diluted Alcohol..........................One-and-a-half Pints.

Dose—One to one-and-a-half drams.

ARNICA MONTANA.

Leopard's-bane.

This plant is a native of the mountainous districts of Europe and Siberia. The flowers, leaves and root are employed in medicine, though the leaves are usually preferred.

MEDICAL PROPERTIES.

Arnica is a stimulant in adynamic diseases; in large doses, taken internally, it causes nausea, vomiting and inflammation of the alimentary canal; in small doses, it increases the perspiration and accelerates the pulse. Is used as a tonic in rheumatism and diseases of the bladder, but more particularly as a domestic remedy in sprains, bruises, rheumatism and local inflammation.

PREPARATION.

Fluid Extract..................................Dose, 10 to 60 Drops.

TINCTURE OF ARNICA.

Fluid Extract............................Two Ounces.
Diluted Alcohol..........................One Pint.

Used externally as a liniment.

INFUSION OF ARNICA.

Fluid Extract..............................One Ounce.
Water......................................One Pint.

Dose—Four to eight drams.

COMPOUND INFUSION OF ARNICA.

Fluid Extract of Arnica....................One Dram.
" " Chamomile................Half Ounce.
" " Peppermint...............Two Drams.
Water......................................Nine Ounces.

Dose—Half to one ounce.

FOMENTATION OF ARNICA.

Fluid Extract of Arnica....................Half Ounce.
Boiling Vinegar............................Five-and-a-half Ounces.
Carbonate of Ammonia.......................Two Drams.

Used as a warm fomentation for the scrotum.

FOMENTATION OF ARNICA AND RUE.

Fluid Extract of Arnica....................Two Ounces.
" " Rue......................One Ounce.
Water......................................Nine Ounces.

Useful in contusions.

ARNICA MIXTURE.

Fluid Extract of Arnica....................Two Drams.
" " Serpentaria..............Two Drams.
Syrup......................................One Dram.
Oil of Peppermint..........................Ten Drops.

Dose—Quarter dram every two hours in the diarrhea complicating typhoid fevers.

ARTEMISIA ABSINTHIUM.

Wormwood.

A native of Europe, but cultivated in this country. The whole plant has a strong bitter odor, and an intensely bitter, aromatic taste. The tops and leaves are used in medicine.

MEDICAL PROPERTIES.

Anthelmintic, tonic and narcotic. Used in intermittent fever, jaundice and worms. Promotes the appetite in atonic dyspepsia, amenorrhea, obstinate diarrhea, &c. Externally, it is useful in fomentations for bruises and local inflammations.

PREPARATIONS.

Fluid Extract..............................Dose, 1-3 to 2-3 Drams.
Solid Extract.............................. " 3 to 5 Grains.

TINCTURE OF WORMWOOD.

Fluid Extract.............. .... Two Ounces.
Diluted Alcohol..............................Fourteen Ounces.
Dose—Two to four drams.

WINE OF WORMWOOD.

Fluid Extract..............................Four Ounces.
Sherry Wine...... ....One Pint.
Dose—One-and-a-half to three drams.

SYRUP OF WORMWOOD.

Fluid Extract..............................Two Ounces.
Syrup ....Six Ounces.
Dose—One to two drams.

FOMENTATION OF WORMWOOD.

Fluid Extract..............................Four Ounces.
Water.................. ....Twelve Ounces.

ASCLEPIAS INCARNATA.

White Indian Hemp.

A native of the United States. The root is officinal.

MEDICAL PROPERTIES.

Emetic, cathartic and diuretic. Useful in catarrh, asthma, rheumatism, syphilis and worms.

PREPARATIONS.

Fluid Extract..............................Dose, 20 to 40 Drops.
Solid Extract.............................. " 3 to 5 Grains.

TINCTURE OF ASCLEPIAS INC.

Fluid Extract....................................Two Ounces.
Diluted Alcohol....................................One Pint.

Dose—One-and-a-half to three drams.

INFUSION OF ASCLEPIAS INC.

Fluid Extract....................................One Ounce.
Water....................................One Pint.

Dose—Three to six drams.

SYRUP OF ASCLEPIAS INC.

Fluid Extract....................................Four Ounces.
Syrup....................................Twelve Ounces.

Dose—Half to one-and-a half drams.

ASCLEPIAS TUBEROSA.

Pleurisy Root

This species is indigenous; most abundant in the Southern States. The root is the only part used in medicine.

MEDICAL PROPERTIES.

The Pleurisy Root is carminative, tonic and diuretic; used in pleurisy, pneumonia, catarrh, febrile diseases, acute rheumatism and dysentery. Administered warm in infusion, to promote diaphoresis, without increasing the temperature of the body. Efficient in flatulency and indigestion.

The Asclepidin has been successfully used in the treatment of affections of the serous membranes, fevers of every type, inflammatory diseases, hooping cough and chronic diseases of the digestive organs.

PREPARATIONS.

Fluid Extract....................................Dose, 1-2 to 2 Drams.
Asclepidin.................................... " 1 to 5 Grains.
Pills ....1 Grain each.

TINCTURE OF PLEURISY ROOT.

Fluid Extract....................................Four Ounces.
Alcohol....................................One Pint.

Dose—Three to five drams.

INFUSION OF PLEURISY ROOT.

Fluid Extract................................One Ounce.
Water..One Pint.

Dose—One to four ounces.

COMPOUND SYRUP OF PLEURISY ROOT.

Fluid Extract of Pleurisy Root................Two Drams.
" " Spearmint.................. " "
" " Sumach.................... " "
" " Bayberry...................One Dram.
" " Black Cohosh................ " "
" " Ginger.....................Half "
Syrup.............................. ......Twenty-four Ounces.

Dose—Two to four drams.

SYRUP OF PLEURISY ROOT.

Fluid Extract................................Four Ounces.
Syrup..Twelve Ounces.

Dose—Quarter to one ounce.

Asclepidin...................................Ten Grains.
Dioscorein................................... " "

Dose—Two to four grains. Beneficial in flatulency, borborygmi and in cases of flatulent and bilious colic.

ASPIDIUM FILIX MAS.

Male Fern.

Said to be nearly universally indigenous. The rhizoma is the officinal part. For its interesting history see U. S. Dispensatory.

MEDICAL PROPERTIES.

Its specific property is anthelmintic. The accounts of its efficacy in the treatment of tapeworm are too numerous to admit of any reasonable doubt on the subject.

PREPARATIONS.

Solid Extract.............. ....Dose, 9 to 15 Grains.
Pills...2 Grains each.

COMPOUND PILLS OF MALE FERN.

Solid Extract of Male Fern........................Two Scruples.
Gamboge..................................Fourteen Grains.
Calomel..................................." "
Scammony..................................Eighteen "

Mix, and divide into twenty pills. In tape-worm.—*Cadet*

ATROPA BELLADONNA.

Belladonna.

This plant is a native of Europe, though it grows vigorously, retaining all its activity, under cultivation, in this country. All the parts are active. The leaves are the only part directed by the U. S. Pharmacopeia.

MEDICAL PROPERTIES.

Belladonna is a powerful narcotic, possessing also diaphoretic and diuretic properties. Exceedingly valuable in convulsions, neuralgia, hooping-cough, rheumatism, gout, paralysis and similar diseases having their seat chiefly in the nervous system. It is esteemed as a prophylactic in scarlatina, as also used with success in quinsy and hernia.

PREPARATIONS.

Fluid Extract.................................Dose, 3 to 10 Drops.
Solid Extract................................." 1-4 to 1 Grain.
Pills...1-4, 1-2, and 1 Grain.
Pills of Atropia..............................1-32 Grain each.

TINCTURE OF BELLADONNA.

Fluid Extract.................................Four Ounces.
Diluted Alcohol...............................Two Pints.

Dose—twenty to forty drops.

INFUSION OF BELLADONNA.

Fluid Extract.................................One Dram.
Water...One Pint.
Compound Tincture of Cardamom.................One Ounce.

Dose—Five drams.

SYRUP OF BELLADONNA.

Fluid Extract.................................One Ounce.
Syrup...Two Pints.

Dose—One to two drams. Useful in hooping-cough.

PILLS OF BELLADONNA, CAMPHOR, ETC.

Camphor....................................Three Drams.
Assafœtida.................................. " "
Solid Extract of Belladonna.................. One Dram.
Opium ....Fifteen Grains.
Syrup of Gum Arabic......... ....Sufficient.

Mix, and make into 120 pills.

Give one pill the first day, two the second, and so on until six are given daily, in hysteria.

COMPOUND BELLADONNA PILLS.

Solid Extract Belladonna.......................Three Grains.
Blue Mass.....................................Twelve "
Powdered Ipecac.............................. " "

Mix, and make twelve pills.

Dose—One, morning and evening.

OINTMENT OF BELLADONNA.

Solid Extract of Belladonna....................One Dram.
Lard ....One Ounce.

Mix.

LINIMENT OF BELLADONNA.

Fluid Extract of Belladonna....................One Dram.
Sulphuric Ether.............................. " "
Cherry Laurel Water...........................Two Ounces.

POULTICE IN NEURALGIA.

Flaxseed meal, combined with two drams of the following mixture:

Fluid Extract of Belladonna....................Six Drams.
" " Opium......................... " "
Powdered Camphor...........................Two "
Water.......................................Six "

Trousseau.

AURANTII CORTEX.

Orange Peel.

Rind of the fruit of *Citrus Vulgaris*. Various parts of the orange tree are used in medicine.

MEDICAL PROPERTIES.

It is a mild tonic, carminative and stomachic, but is seldom used alone. It is a useful addition to bitter infusions and decoctions.

PREPARATION.

Fluid Extract.................................Dose, 1-2 to 2 Drams.

TINCTURE OF ORANGE PEEL.

Fluid Extract..........................Three-and-a-half Ounces.
Diluted Alcohol........................Two Pints.

Used principally as an addition to infusions, decoctions, &c.

SYRUP OF ORANGE PEEL.

Fluid Extract..........................Two Ounces.
Syrup..................................Fourteen Ounces.

Used mainly as an agreeable drink mixed with water.

MIXTURE OF ORANGE PEEL.

Fluid Extract of Orange Peel.............Half Dram.
" " Canella................. " "
" " Colombo................ " "
Syrup..................................One-and-a-half Ounces.

Dose—One to three drams in habitual diarrhea.

BAPTISIA TINCTORIA.

Wild Indigo.

This is a small shrub, found in most parts of the United States. The root and leaves are medicinal. The virtue seems to reside in the bark.

MEDICAL PROPERTIES.

Principally used on account of its antiseptic virtues. It is an excellent application as a wash or gargle to all species of ulcers, as malignant ulcerous sore mouth and throat, mercurial sore mouth, scrofulous or syphilitic opthalmia, &c. Internally it acts powerfully on the glandular and nervous systems, increasing all the glandular secretions and arousing the liver especially to a normal action.

PREPARATIONS.

Fluid Extract.................................Dose, 1-4 to 1-2 Dram.
Baptisin...................................... " 1-4 to 1-2 Grain.

TINCTURE OF WILD INDIGO.

Fluid Extract..........................Two Ounces.
Diluted Alcohol........................One Pint.

Dose—Two to four drams.

INFUSION OF WILD INDIGO

Fluid Extract...... ....One Ounce.
Water.......................................One Pint.

Dose—Half ounce every four hours.

Comstock.

GARGLE OF WILD INDIGO.

Fluid Extract..................................Four Ounces.
Water.......................................Twelve Ounces.

BAROSMA CRENATA.

Buchu.

The Barosma plants grow at the Cape of Good Hope. The leaves are medicinal.

MEDICAL PROPERTIES.

Buchu is given chiefly in complaints of the urinary organs attended with increased uric acid, as gravel, chronic catarrh of the bladder, morbid irritation of the bladder and urethra, diseases of the prostate and retention or incontinence of urine from a loss of tone in the parts concerned in its evacuation; also in dyspepsia, chronic rheumatism, cutaneous affections and dropsy.

PREPARATIONS.

Fluid Extract of Buchu.........................Dose, 1-2 to 2 Drams.
" " " Compound .... " 1-2 to 2 Drams.

TINCTURE OF BUCHU.

Fluid Extract............................. ...Two Ounces.
Diluted Alcohol..................................One Pint.

Dose—Half to one ounce.

INFUSION OF BUCHU.

Fluid Extract..................................One Ounce.
Water ....One Pint.

Dose—One to two Ounces.

MIXTURE OF BUCHU AND ACETATE OF POTASH.

Fluid Extract of Buchu.........................Half Ounce.
Acetate of Potash.................... ....Two Drams.
Water.......................................Eight Ounces.

Dose—Four ounces, three or four times a day.

This is an excellent diuretic combination, and its value may be farther enhanced by the addition of Sweet Spirits of Nitre.

BUCHU COMPOUND.

A combination of Buchu, Uva Ursi, Juniper, and Cubebs.

INFUSION OF BUCHU COMPOUND.

Fluid Extract of Buchu Compound............Four Ounces.
Water..................................Twelve Ounces.

Dose—Two drams to one ounce.

COMPOUND INFUSION OF BUCHU, UVA URSI AND SENEKA.

Fluid Extract of Buchu....................Half Ounce.
" " Uva Ursi.................. " "
" " Seneka.................. " "
Water..................................Eight Ounces.

Dose—One to two drams every two hours in atony of the bladder and mucous discharges.

CANELLA ALBA.

Canella.

A native of Jamaica and other West India islands. The bark is the part employed in medicine.

MEDICAL PROPERTIES.

Canella is possessed of the ordinary properties of aromatics; acting as a local stimulant and gentle tonic, producing upon the stomach a warming cordial effect, which makes it valuable as an addition to tonic or purgative medicines in debilitated states of the digestive organs. Seldom prescribed except in combinations.

PREPARATION.

Fluid Extract..............................Dose, 15 to 30 Drops.

TINCTURE OF CANELLA.

Fluid Extract..............................Six Drams.
Diluted Alcohol............................Eight Ounces.

Dose—One-and-a-half to three drams.

TINCTURE OF HIERA PICRA.

Fluid Extract of Canella....................One-and-a-half Ounces.
Aloes....................................One-and-a-half Ounces.
Brandy.....................................One Pint.

Dose—One dram, three times a day in amenorrhea.

WINE OF ALOES AND CANELLA.

Socotrine Aloes (rubbed to powder)...........Two Ounces.
Fluid Extract of Canella....................Four Drams.
Sherry Wine.............................Two Pints.

Dose—As a stomachic, one to two drams; as a purgative, half to two ounces.

See Wine of Gentian.

CANNABIS INDICA.

Indian Hemp, Foreign

The true Cannabis Indica is imported from India. It is cultivated largely in parts of Europe and Asia.

MEDICAL PROPERTIES.

Phrenic, anæsthetic, anti-spasmodic and hypnotic. Unlike opium, it does not constipate the bowels, lessen the appetite, create nausea, produce dryness of the tongue, check pulmonary secretions or produce headache. Used with success in hysteria, chorea, gout, neuralgia, acute and sub-acute rheumatism, tetanus, hydrophobia and the like.

PREPARATIONS.

Fluid Extract.....................................Dose, 5 to 10 Drops.
Solid Extract..................................." 1 to 2 Grains.
Pills...Half and One Grain.

TINCTURE OF CANNABIS INDICA.

Fluid Extract...........................Half Ounce.
Alcohol..........................Twelve Ounces.

Dose—Half to one dram, and gradually increased in *tetanus* every half hour until the paroxysms cease or catalepsy is induced.

DRAUGHT OF CANNABIS INDICA.

Tincture of Cannabis Indica.................Half Dram.
Camphor Mixture.........................One-and-a-half Ounces.

Aromatic Spirits of Ammonia...... .. ..Half Dram.

To be taken at bed-time. As a substitute for opium and its preparations, to relieve pain, induce sleep, &c.—*Clendinning*.

SYRUP OF CANNABIS INDICA.

Fluid Extract..................................One Ounce.

Syrup..One Pint.

Dose—Twenty-five to fifty drops.

MIXTURE OF CANNABIS INDICA.

Fluid Extract of Cannabis.........................One Ounce.

" " Ignatia.........................One Ounce.

Dose—Five to fifteen drops.

WINE OF CANNABIS INDICA.

Fluid Extract..................................Six Drams.

Sherry Wine....................................One Pint.

Dose—Half to one dram.

PILLS OF CANNABIS AND IGNATIA.

Solid Extract of Cannabis Indica..................Twelve Grains.

" " Ignatia.........................Nine Grains.

Make into twelve pills.

Dose—One.

CAPSICUM ANNUUM.

Cayenne Pepper.

This plant is a native of the East Indies, though it is extensively cultivated in this country and in Europe. The fruit is officinal.

MEDICAL PROPERTIES.

A powerful stimulant, and a condiment; is very useful in correcting flatulency in dyspepsia, promoting digestion, in sea-sickness on the first occasion of nausea, in dropsies, in malignant sore throat and scarlet fever as a gargle, in intermittents with Quinine, and low forms of fever, in cholera, and in hot climates for obviating the black vomit.

PREPARATION.

Fluid Extract..................................Dose, 5 to 15 Drops.

Pills..1 Grain each.

TINCTURE OF CAYENNE PEPPER.

Fluid Extract..................................One Ounce.
Diluted Alcohol..................................One Pint.

Dose—One to two drams. Used in low states of fever with gastric insensibility, also when diluted, as a gargle.

INFUSION OF CAYENNE PEPPER.

Fluid Extract..................................Half Ounce.
Boiling Water..................................One Pint.

Dose—Two to four drams.

GARGLE OF CAYENNE PEPPER.

Fluid Extract..................................One Ounce.
Common Salt..................................One Dram.
Boiling Vinegar..................................One Pint.
" Water..................................One Pint.

Used as a gargle in bad cases of scarlatina.

SYRUP OF CAYENNE PEPPER

Fluid Extract..................................Half Ounce.
Syrup..................................Eight Ounces.

Dose—One to two drams.

CASSIA ACUTIFOLIA.

Senna.

The Cassia grows in great abundance in Upper Egypt, and probably in other parts of Africa. The leaves are the parts used in medicine.

MEDICAL PROPERTIES.

It is well adapted to cases which require an active and certain purgative; in constipation and inactivity of the alimentary canal, requiring frequent use of purgatives; in worms; in determination of the blood to the head. It can be used by persons of all ages as a purgative, with security.

PREPARATIONS.

Fluid Extract..................................	Dose,	1 to 2 Drams.
" " Aqueous..................................	"	1 to 2 Drams.
" " Senna and Jalap..................................	"	1-2 to 1 Dram.
Solid Extract..................................	"	3 to 8 Grains.
Pills..................................	"	2 Grains each.

TINCTURE OF SENNA.

Fluid Extract..............................Three Ounces.
Diluted Alcohol.............................Thirteen Ounces.
Dose—Half to one ounce.

INFUSION OF SENNA.

Fluid Extract............... ... .Two Ounces.
Water....................................One Pint.
Dose—One to two ounces.

SYRUP OF SENNA.

Fluid Extract..............................Four Ounces.
Essence of Fennel..........................One Dram.
Syrup......................................Ten Ounces.
Dose—Half to one ounce.

SENNA MIXTURE.

Fluid Extract of Senna................ .....Half Dram.
" " " Jalap.. ....Eighteen Drops.
" " " Ginger......................Sixteen Drops.
Sulphate of Magnesia.................... ..Four Drams.
Diluted Alcohol............................One Dram.
Water...................... ....One Ounce.
Mix. As a purgative draught.

CEPHAELIS IPECACUANHA.

Ipecac.

This plant is a native of Brazil. The root is the officinal portion.

MEDICAL PROPERTIES.

It is a mild and tolerably certain emetic, and being usually thrown from the stomach in one or two efforts, it is not apt to produce dangerous effects. It is especially useful when poisons have been swallowed, in cases of dysentery, as a nauseate in asthma, hooping-cough and the hemorrhages, and as an expectorant in catarrhal and other pulmonary affections.

PREPARATIONS.

Fluid Extract......................Dose, { Expectorant, 5 to 10 Drops. / Emetic, 1-2 to 1 Dram. }
Pills of Ipecac..................................Quarter Grain each.
" " Dov. P., (1-2 gr. Op., 1-2 gr. Ip., 1 gr. Sul. Pot.) Two Grains each.
" " Ipecac and Squill.........................Three Grains each.

TINCTURE OF IPECAC.

Fluid Extract..............................Two Ounces.
Diluted Alcohol.............................Two Pints.

Dose—Three-quarters to one-and-a-half or two drams.

WINE OF IPECAC.

Fluid Extract.................. ....Three Ounces.
Sherry Wine.................... ....One Pint.

Dose—Quarter to half dram, and two-and-a-half to five ounces.

SYRUP OF IPECAC.

Fluid Extract.......................... ...Two Ounces.
Syrup.....................................Fourteen Ounces.

Dose—Half to one dram, and half to one ounce.

IPECAC EXPECTORANT FOR YOUNG CHILDREN.

Fluid Extract of Ipecac......................Two Drams.
Syrup of Tolu. ....Five Drams
Mucilage..................................One Ounce.
Sherry Wine................................Three Drams.

Dose—One dram.

MIXTURE OF IPECAC.

Fluid Extract of Ipecac.....................Half Dram.
" " " Squill..........................One Dram.
Tartrate of Antimony and Potassa............One Grain.
Diluted Alcohol............................Seven Drams.
Distilled Water............................Seven Ounces.

Dose—Two ounces at first, afterwards one ounce every ten minutes until vomiting is induced.

This mixture is recommended in dropsies previously to giving digitalis.

Ellis.

CHELIDONIUM MAJUS.

Great Celandine.

Celandine is indigenous to Europe, and is extensively naturalized in the United States. The root is more powerful than the stem, and is usually preferred.

MEDICAL PROPERTIES.

As a drastic hydragogue, fully equal to gamboge. Useful in hepatic affections, and is supposed to exert a special influence on the spleen. Applied in the form of a poultice to scrofulous and cutaneous diseases and piles; also to indolent ulcers, fungous growths, &c.

PREPARATIONS.

Fluid Extract..................................Dose, 10 to 20 Drops.
Solid Extract.................................. " 5 to 10 Grains.

TINCTURE OF CELANDINE.

Fluid Extract............................Two Ounces.
Diluted Alcohol..... ....One Pint.
Dose—Three-quarters to one-and-a-half drams.

EXTRACT OF CELANDINE MIXTURE.

Fluid Extract of Celandine ....Two-and-a-half Drams.
" " " Henbane.................Half Dram.
Sulphate of Potassa.......................One Ounce.
Tartar Emetic............................One Grain.
Elder Water..............................Six Ounces.
Oxymel of Squill.........................One Ounce.
Dose—Two to three drams every two hours as a hydragogue.

Augustin.

INFUSION OF CELANDINE.

Fluid Extract............................Half Ounce.
Water....................................One Pint.
Dose—Two-and-a-half to five drams.

SYRUP OF CELANDINE.

Fluid Extract............................Three Ounces.
Syrup....................................One Pint.

CHELONE GLABRA.

Balmony.

Found in wet situations in the United States. The leaves, which are exceedingly bitter, but inodorous, are the parts used in medicine.

MEDICAL PROPERTIES.

Tonic, cathartic and anthelmintic. Valuable in jaundice and hepatic diseases, likewise for the removal of worms. Used as a tonic in small doses, in dyspepsia, debility of the digestive organs, and during convalescence from febrile and inflammatory diseases.

PREPARATIONS.

Fluid Extract....................................Dose, 1 Dram.
Chelonin.. " 1 to 2 Grains.

TINCTURE OF BALMONY.

Fluid Extract..................................One Ounce.
Diluted Alcohol................................Eight Ounces.
Dose—One to two drams.

SYRUP OF BALMONY.

Fluid Extract..................................Half Ounce.
Syrup..Twelve Ounces.
Dose—Three to five drams.

CHIMAPHILA UMBELLATA.

Pipsissewa. Prince's Pine.

This is a small evergreen plant, growing in the northern latitudes of this country, Europe and Asia. The whole plant is endowed with active properties.

MEDICAL PROPERTIES.

Tonic, diuretic and astringent. Highly recommended in dropsy; useful in disordered digestion and general debility, rheumatism and nephritic affections, scrofula, in obstinate, ill-conditioned ulcers, in cutaneous eruptions, and in chronic affections of the urinary organs.

PREPARATIONS.

Fluid Extract....................................Dose, 1 Dram.
Solid Extract.................................... " 10 to 20 Grains.
Pills—Three grains each.

INFUSION OF PRINCE'S PINE.

Fluid Extract..................................One Ounce.
Water..One Pint.
Dose—Two ounces.

INFUSION OF PRINCE'S PINE AND SENNA.

Fluid Extract of Prince's Pine................Six Drams.
" " " Senna......................Two Drams.
Water....................................Twelve Ounces.
Dose—Half to one ounce.

SYRUP OF PRINCE'S PINE.

Fluid Extract..............................Four Ounces.
Syrup......................................Twelve Ounces
Dose—Half ounce. *Wm. Procter.*

CIMICIFUGA RACEMOSA.

Black Cohosh.

Native of the United States. The root is the part employed.

MEDICAL PROPERTIES.

This remedy possesses an undoubted influence over the nervous system, and has been successfully used in chorea, epilepsy, nervous excitability, asthma, delirium tremens, and many spasmodic affections. In febrile diseases it frequently produces diaphoresis and diuresis. The Cimicifugin does not possess the narcotic properties of the root. It is antiperiodic, nervine, tonic, with an especial affinity for the uterus.

PREPARATIONS.

Fluid Extract of Black Cohosh..................Dose, 1-2 to 2 Drams.
" " " " Compound........ " 1-2 to 1 Dram.
Solid Extract................................ " 4 to 8 Grains.
Cimicifugin.................................. " 1 to 6 Grains.
Pills of Cimicifugin............................1 Grain each.
" " Ext. Cimicifuga.......................2 Grains each.

TINCTURE OF BLACK COHOSH.

Fluid Extract..............................Four Ounces.
Diluted Alcohol............................One Pint.
Dose—Two-and-a-half to five drams.

COMPOUND TINCTURE OF BLACK COHOSH.

Fluid Extract of Black Cohosh...............One Ounce.
" " " Blood Root.................Half Ounce.

Fluid Extract of Poke ....Two Drams.
Alcohol ....One Pint.

Dose—Half to one dram. Used in pulmonary affections, hepatic diseases, dyspepsia, &c.

SYRUP OF BLACK COHOSH.

Fluid Extract ....Three Ounces.
Syrup ....Six Ounces.

Dose—Half to one dram.

COMPOUND PILLS OF BLACK COHOSH.

Solid Extract of Black Cohosh ....One Dram.
" " " Scullcap ....One Dram.
Valerianate of Quinia ....Half Dram.

Make 60 pills. Dose—One every two or three hours. Used in nervous diseases, chorea and fevers attended with wakefulness or restlessness.

Cimicifugin ....10 Grains.
Dioscorein ....8 Grains.

Dose—Three to five grains, in flatulency and to remove the tendency to bilious colic.

BLACK COHOSH COMPOUND.

Compound of Black Cohosh, Wild Cherry, Ipecac, Liquorice, Seneka.

SYRUP OF BLACK COHOSH COMPOUND.

Fluid Extract ....Two Ounces.
Syrup ....One Pint.

Dose—Three to six drams.

CINCHONA.

Peruvian Bark.

The genuine cinchona trees are confined exclusively to South America. Those that yield the bark of commerce grow at various elevations upon the Andes: seldom less than 4,000 feet above the level of the sea.

MEDICAL PROPERTIES.

Valuable in functional derangements of the stomach, improving digestion, and invigorating the nervous and muscular systems in diseases of general debility, and in convalescence from exhausting diseases. As a tonic it will be found of advantage in measles, small-pox, scarlatina during the absence of fever or inflammation, also in cases when the system is exhausted by purulent discharges. It may likewise be used in all chronic diseases attended with debility, as scrofula, dropsy, obstinate cutaneous diseases, &c. To obtain the antiperiodic influence the red and yellow barks are considered superior to the pale, while the pale is preferred as a tonic.

PREPARATIONS.

Fluid Extract of Cinchona........................Dose, 1-2 to 1 Dram.
" " " " Compound............. " 1-2 to 1 Dram.

TINCTURE OF CINCHONA.

Fluid Extract, (yellow bark,)...................Four Ounces.
Diluted Alcohol...................................One Pint
Dose—One to four drams.

INFUSION OF CINCHONA.

Fluid Extract, (yellow bark,)...................One Ounce.
Water...One Pint.
Dose—One to two ounces.
Tincture and Infusion of the Red Bark prepared in the same way.

COMPOUND INFUSION OF CINCHONA.

Fluid Extract of Cinchona......................One Ounce.
" " " Snake Root...................Half Ounce.
" " " Orange Peel..................Two Drams.
" " " Cloves........................One Dram.
Carbonate of Potassa..........................One Dram.
Water...One Pint.
Dose—One to one-and-a-half ounces.

COMPOUND TINCTURE OF CINCHONA.

Fluid Extract of Red Bark......................Four Ounces.
" " " Orange Peel........ ....One-and-a-half Oz.
" " " Snake Root...................Three Drams.
" " " Saffron........................One Dram.
Red Saunders..................................One Dram.
Diluted Alcohol..............................Twenty Ounces.
Dose—One to two Drams.

WINE OF CINCHONA.

Fluid Extract.................................Six Ounces.
Sherry Wine..................................Ten Ounces.
Dose—One-and-a-half to three drams.

MIXTURE OF CINCHONA AND VALERIAN.

Fluid Extract of Cinchona...... ....One Ounce.
" " " Valerian.....................One Ounce.
Essence of Cardamom......................Two Drams.
Dose—One dram every three hours, as a tonic in nervous temperaments.

MIXTURE OF CINCHONA AND CHAMOMILE.

Fluid Extract of Cinchona....................Half Ounce.
" " " Chamomile.................Half Ounce.
" " " Orange Peel................Half Ounce.
Syrup.......................................Four Ounces.
Water.......................................Two-and-a-half Oz.

Dose—One to four drams every two or three hours. In anæmia of children, atrophy from bad diet, &c.

CINCHONA COMPOUND.

Compounded of CINCHONA, ORANGE PEEL, GENTIAN, SERPENTARIA, CLOVES and RED SAUNDERS.

CISSAMPELOS PAREIRA.

Pareira Brava.

Native of the West Indies and South America. The root is the part used in medicine.

MEDICAL PROPERTIES.

Useful in calculous affections, diseases of the urinary passages, chronic inflammation and ulceration of the kidneys and bladder. It allays irritability of the bladder, and corrects the disposition to profuse mucous secretions.

PREPARATIONS.

Fluid Extract................................Dose, 1-2 to 1 Dram.

TINCTURE OF PAREIRA BRAVA.

Fluid Extract..............................Three Ounces.
Diluted Alcohol...........................Thirteen Ounces.
Dose—Two to four drams.

INFUSION OF PAREIRA BRAVA.

Fluid Extract..............................Six Drams.
Water ....One Pint.
Dose—One to two ounces.

COCCULUS PALMATUS.

Colombo.

This plant grows abundantly on the south-eastern coast of Africa, in the neighborhood of Mozambique, where it is known by the name of *Ralumb*. The root is the officinal portion.

MEDICAL PROPERTIES.

Mild tonic. Used in simple dyspepsia; in those states of debility which attend convalescence from acute disorders, particularly in enfeebled condition of the alimentary canal, in dysentery, cholera morbus and cholera infantum.

PREPARATIONS.

Fluid Extract ....Dose, 20 to 60 Drops.
Solid Extract.................................... " 4 to 10 Grains.
Pills ....2 Grains each.

TINCTURE OF COLOMBO.

Fluid Extract....................................Two Ounces.
Diluted Alcohol................................One Pint.
Dose—One-and-a-half to four drams.

INFUSION OF COLOMBO.

Fluid Extract....................................One Ounce.
Water...One Pint.
Dose—Three drams to one ounce.

WINE OF COLOMBO.

Fluid Extract....................................One Ounce.
Sherry Wine......................................Ten Ounces.
Dose—Two to four drams.

COMPOUND INFUSION OF COLOMBO.

1.

Fluid Extract of Colombo.........................One Dram.
" " Orange Peel......................Four Drams.
Water...One Ounce.
Dose—Two drams every hour in atony of the intestines, manifesting itself by diarrhea.—*M. Hauner.*

2.

Fluid Extract of Colombo..........................One Ounce.
" " Ginger..........................Two Drams.
Water ....One Pint.

Dose—Two ounces every two hours in chronic diarrhea.

3.

Fluid Extract of Colombo..........................One Dram.
" " Rhubarb..........................One "
" " Ginger..........................Half "
Water ....One Pint.

Dose—One dram in diarrhea.

PILLS OF COLOMBO AND TARTRATE OF POTASSA AND IRON.

Tartrate of Potassa and Iron......................Two Ounces.
Solid Extract of Colombo..........................One Ounce.

Make four grain pills. Dose—Two to four.

MIXTURE OF COLOMBO AND CASCARILLA.

Fluid Extract of Colombo..........................Half Ounce.
" " Cascarilla ....Two Drams.
Tincture of Orange Peel.......................... " "
Syrup of Cinnamon.................................One Ounce.
Water ....Six Ounces.

Dose—One dram, every hour, in chronic diarrhea.—*Berends.*

COMPOUND PILLS OF COLOMBO.

Solid Extract of Colombo..........................One Dram.
" " Rhubarb ....Two Scruples.
" " Chamomile........................Two Drams.
Oil of Caraway....................................Five Drops.
Syrup of Saffron..................................Sufficient.

Make into four grain pills.

Dose—Four a day in mania, with amenorrhea.

COLCHICUM AUTUMNALE.

Colchicum.

Native of the temperate parts of Europe. The roots and seeds are officinal.

MEDICAL PROPERTIES.

Colchicum is principally used in the various forms of gout and rheumatism, in which experience has abundantly proved it to be a highly valuable remedy. It is also recommended in inflammatory and febrile diseases, diseases of the heart, in various nervous complaints, as chorea, hysteria, and hypochondriasis, and chronic bronchial affections.

PREPARATIONS.

Fluid Extract of Colchicum Root..................Dose, 3 to 12 Drops.
" " " " Seed.................. " 5 to 15 Drops.
Pills..1-2 Grain each.

TINCTURE OF COLCHICUM SEED.

Fluid Extract................................Four Ounces.
Diluted Alcohol..............................Twelve Ounces.
Dose—Ten drops to half dram.

SYRUP OF COLCHICUM SEED.

Fluid Extract................................Two Ounces.
Syrup...... ....Fourteen Ounces.
Dose—One-third to one dram.

WINE OF COLCHICUM SEED.

Fluid Extract................................Three Ounces.
Sherry Wine..................................One Pint.
Dose—Thirty drops to half dram.

A Tincture, Syrup, and Wine, may be prepared from the Fluid Extract of Colchicum Root in the same way and administered in the like doses.

COMPOUND TINCTURE OF COLCHICUM SEED.

Fluid Extract................................Three Ounces.
Aromatic Spirits of Ammonia..................One Pint.
Dose—Ten to twenty drops.

TINCTURE OF COLCHICUM AND DIGITALIS.

Fluid Extract of Colchicum Seed................Half Dram.
" " " Digitalis......................Half Dram.
Nitric Ether.................................One Dram.
Diluted Alcohol..............................Three Drams.
Dose—Ten to fifteen drops.

MIXTURE OF COLCHICUM.

Wine of Colchicum..........................One Ounce.
Fluid Extract of Opium......................Half Dram.
Syrup.......................................Two Ounces.
Dose—Two to three drams.

CONIUM MACULATUM.

Poison Hemlock.

Native of Europe and Asia, and is naturalized in many parts of the United States. The leaves and seeds are officinal.

MEDICAL PROPERTIES.

Powerful narcotic. Anodyne, anti-spasmodic and deobstruent. Used in chronic enlargement of the liver, chronic rheumatism, syphilis, neuralgic affections, asthma, &c.

PREPARATIONS.

Fluid Extract..............................Dose, 5 to 20 Drops.
Solid Extract..............................“ 1-2 to 1 1-2 Grains.
Pills......................................1-4, 1-2 and 1 Grain.
Pills of Conium and Ipecac.................1 Grain each.

TINCTURE OF CONIUM.

Fluid Extract..............................Three Ounces.
Diluted Alcohol............................One Pint.
Dose—Thirty drops to a dram.

INFUSION OF CONIUM.

Fluid Extract..............................Half Ounce.
Water......................................One Pint.
Used as a wash in cancerous and malignant ulcers.

MIXTURE OF CONIUM AND POPPY.

Fluid Extract of Conium....................Half Dram.
“ “ “ Poppy................................Two Drams.
Syrup......................................Six Drams.
Water......................................Seven Ounces.
Dose—Half ounce, three or four times a day.

PILLS OF CONIUM AND IPECAC.

Solid Extract of Conium ....Five Drams.
Powdered Ipecac.............................One Dram.

Make into one grain pills. Dose—One to two at bed time, in pulmonary irritations, with rheumatic and other pains.

PILLS OF CONIUM AND CALOMEL.

Solid Extract of Conium.......................Thirty Grains.
Calomel.......................................Fifteen Grains.

Mix well and form twenty pills. Dose—One three times a day in syphiloid diseases.

OINTMENT OF CONIUM.

Solid Extract of Conium......................One Ounce.
Lard...Four Ounces.

As an application to scrofulous ulcers.

CORNUS FLORIDA.

Boxwood. Dogwood.

Indigenous, yet most abundant in the Middle States. The bark is the medicinal portion.

MEDICAL PROPERTIES.

Tonic, astringent and stimulant. Its internal use increases the force and frequency of the pulse and elevates the temperature of the body. It has been successfully substituted for cinchona in the treatment of intermittents.

PREPARATIONS.

Fluid Extract...............................	Dose,	1-2 to 2 Drams.
Solid Extract...............................	"	5 to 10 Grains.
Cornin......................................	"	1 to 10 Grains.
Pills of Cornus and Cornin..................	"	2 Grains each.

TINCTURE OF DOGWOOD.

Fluid Extract................................Four Ounces.
Diluted Alcohol..............................Twelve Ounces.

Dose—Two to four drams.

INFUSION OF DOGWOOD.

Fluid Extract................................Two Ounces.
Water..One Pint.

Dose—Two ounces every hour.

WINE OF DOGWOOD.

Fluid Extract.................................Five Ounces.
Sherry Wine..................................Ten Ounces.
Dose—One-and-a-half to three drams.

SYRUP OF DOGWOOD.

Fluid Extract.................................Four Ounces.
Syrup...One Pint.
Dose—Two to three drams.

CORYDALIS FORMOSA.

Turkey Corn.

The Corydalis is indigenous; found growing in rich soil, among rocks and old decayed timber, westward and south of New York to North Carolina. The root or tuber, which is a small round ball, is the officinal portion, and should be collected only while the plant is in flower.

MEDICAL PROPERTIES.

One of the best remedies in syphilitic affections; valuable in scrofula, and possesses tonic properties similar to the gentian, colombo, or other pure bitters. Its alterative powers render it of immense value. The Corydalin possesses all the alterative properties of the bulb in an eminent degree; will be found useful in all scrofulous and syphilitic affections, as well as in many cutaneous diseases.

PREPARATIONS.

Fluid Extract.................................Dose, 10 to 40 Drops.
Corydalin..................................... " 1-2 " 1 Grain

TINCTURE OF TURKEY CORN.

Fluid Extract.................................Three Ounces.
Diluted Alcohol...............................One Pint.
Dose—Half to two drams.

COMPOUND SYRUP OF TURKEY CORN

Fluid Extract of Turkey Corn..................Two Ounces.
" " " Blue Flag.....................One Ounce.
Syrup... Eight Ounces.
Dose—Half to one dram.

Corydalin....................................Eight Grains.
Hydrastin....................................Ten Grains.

Mix well, and divide into twelve powders. An excellent alterative in syphilis.

Corydalin....................................Two Grains.
Xanthoxylin....................................Six Grains.

Make into three powders. Used as an alterative in syphilitic and scrofulous affections.

CROCUS SATIVUS.

Saffron.

Saffron is a native of Greece and Asia Minor, and is much cultivated in some parts of Europe. The stigmas of the flower are the officinal parts of the plant.

MEDICAL PROPERTIES.

Emmenagogue and diaphoretic. Has been of benefit in amenorrhea, dysmenorrhea, chlorosis, hysteria, and in suppression of the menstrual discharge. It is a well known domestic remedy in promoting the eruption in exanthematous diseases. It imparts color and flavor to officinal tinctures.

PREPARATION.

Fluid Extract....................................Dose, 20 to 60 Drops.

TINCTURE OF SAFFRON.

Fluid Extract....................................One Ounce.
Diluted Alcohol....................................One Pint.

Dose—Half to one dram.

INFUSION OF SAFFRON.

Fluid Extract....................................Two Drams.
Water....................................Two Pints.

Dose—Two to three ounces.

SYRUP OF SAFFRON.

Fluid Extract....................................Five Drams.
Alcohol....................................Two-and-a-half Oz.
Syrup....................................Twelve Ounces.

Dose—Half to one ounce.

CROTON ELEUTERIA.

Cascarilla.

This shrub grows wild in the West Indies. The bark is officinal.

MEDICAL PROPERTIES.

A pleasant and gentle aromatic and tonic; employed in dyspepsia, chronic diarrhea and dysentery, flatulent colic and other cases of debility of the stomach and bowels, and to arrest vomiting. Cascarilla counteracts the tendency of cinchona to produce nausea.

PREPARATIONS.

Fluid Extract...... ....Dose, 20 to 30 Drops.

TINCTURE OF CASCARILLA.

Fluid Extract................................Five Ounces.
Diluted Alcohol ....Two Pints.
Dose—One dram.

INFUSION OF CASCARILLA.

Fluid Extract................................One Ounce.
Water.......................................One Pint.
Dose—One to three drams.

ALKALINE INFUSION OF CASCARILLA.

Fluid Extract................................Three Ounces.
Carbonate of Potassa...........................Two Drams.
Water.......................................Ten Ounces.
Dose—One dram, as an antacid and tonic.

COMPOUND WINE OF CASCARILLA.

Fluid Extract of Cascarilla.....................One-and-a-half Oz.
" " " Orange Peel.......... ....One Ounce.
Essence of Cinnamon................. ......Two Drams.
White Wine...............................Twenty-seven Oz
Dose—Two ounces, four times a day.

CUCUMIS COLOCYNTHIS.

Colocynth.

Native of Northern Africa. The fruit, deprived of its rind, is the part used in medicine.

MEDICAL PROPERTIES.

Colocynth is a powerful drastic, hydragogue cathartic, exciting inflammation of the mucous membranes of the intestines, causing severe griping, vomiting and bloody discharges. From its powerful and harsh action it is rarely used alone. It is principally useful in passive dropsy, in cerebral derangements, and for the purpose of overcoming torpid conditions of the biliary and digestive systems.

PREPARATIONS.

Solid Extract of Colocynth........................	Dose, 5 to 15 Grains.
" " " " Compound..............	" 2 to 30 "
Pills of Colocynth Compound......................	3 grs. each.
" " " " and Hyoscyamus.......	3 " "
" " " and Blue Pill	3 " "
" " " " Calomel	3 " "

PILLS OF COLOCYNTH AND BLUE MASS.

Blue Mass..............................Five Grains.
Solid Ext. Colocynth Compound............Five Grains.
Oil of Caraway...........................Two Drops.

Make into two pills. These constitute an active cathartic.

PILLS OF COLOCYNTH AND CALOMEL.

Solid Ext. Colocynth Compound............Forty-eight Grains.
Mild Chloride of Mercury.................One Scruple.

Divide into twenty pills. Two or three will generally act as a cathartic

FOTHERGILL'S PILLS.

Solid Ext. Colocynth Compound.........One-and-a-half Drams.
Oxide of Antimony....................Half Dram.

Mix, and divide into thirty pills.

PILLS OF COMPOUND EXTRACT OF COLOCYNTH.

Solid Ext. Colocynth Compound...........One Scruple.
" " Jalap..........................One-and-a-half Scruples.
Powder of Scammony Compound...........Ten Grains.
Mild Chloride of Mercury..................Ten Grains.
Tartrate of Antimony and Potash...........One Grain.
Soap..................................Five Grains.
Oil of Cinnamon..........................Four Drops.

Mix, and divide into fifteen pills. Dose—One, two or three, to be taken at bed time. *Dr. Meigs.*

COLOCYNTH AND HYOSCYAMUS.

Colocynth Compound............................Two Parts.
Extract Hyoscyamus............................One Part.

Divide into three grain pills. Colocynth is deprived of its griping properties by combination with Extract of Hyoscyamus.

CURCUMA LONGA.

Turmeric.

Native of the East Indies and Cochin-China. The rhizoma is the official part.

MEDICAL PROPERTIES.

Stimulant aromatic, tonic, discussive and heating: used especially in the jaundice and the itch, also employed in debilitated states of the stomach, intermittent fever and dropsy.

PREPARATION.

Fluid Extract...................................Dose, 2 to 3 Drams.

TINCTURE OF TURMERIC.

Fluid Extract..................................Two Ounces.
Diluted Alcohol...............................Twelve Ounces.

Dose—One-and-a-half to two ounces.

INFUSION OF TURMERIC.

Fluid Extract..................................One Ounce.
Water..Ten Ounces.

Dose—Two to four ounces.

CYPRIPEDIUM PUBESCENS.

Ladies' Slipper.

This is an indigenous plant. The fibrous roots are the parts used in medicine.

MEDICAL PROPERTIES.

Tonic, nervine, anti-spasmodic. Employed in nervous headache, nervous irritability and excitability, hysteria, neuralgia, morbid condition of the nervous system, &c.

PREPARATIONS

Fluid Extract............................Dose 1-2 to 1 Dram.
Solid Extract............................ " 5 " 15 Grains.
Cypripedin.............................. " 2 " 4 Grains.
Pills.................................... " 2 Grains.

TINCTURE OF LADIES' SLIPPER.

Fluid Extract..................................Two Ounces.
Diluted Alcohol................................One Pint.
Dose—Half to one ounce.

SYRUP OF LADIES' SLIPPER.

Fluid Extract......................... .....Four Ounces.
Syrup...Fourteen Ounces.
Dose—Two to four drams.

COMPOUND PILLS OF LADIES' SLIPPER.

Solid Extract of Ladies' Slipper.................Twelve Grains.
" " " Hops.........................Twelve Grains.
" " " Lettuce.......................Four Grains.
Make into six pills. Dose—One to two.

COMPOUND MIXTURE OF LADIES' SLIPPER.

Fluid Extract of Ladies' Slipper.................One Ounce.
" " " Pleurisy Root.................. " "
" " " Skunk Cabbage................. " "
" " " Scullcap...................... " "
Dose—Half to one dram three times a day.

To allay irritability or excitability of the nervous system, to relieve spasms, and to produce sleep in restless, waking or excited condition.

MIXTURE OF LADIES' SLIPPER, CATNIP AND SCULLCAP.

Fluid extract of Ladies' Slipper.................Half Ounce.
" " " Catnip....................... " "
" " " Scullcap..................... " "
Water...One Pint.
Dose—One-and-a-half to three drams. For sick and nervous headache, not dependent on acid stomach.

DATURA STRAMONIUM.

Stramonium.

This is a well known poisonous weed, growing in all parts of the United States. Almost every part of the plant is possessed of medicinal properties, but the officinal parts are the leaves and seeds.

MEDICAL PROPERTIES.

Narcotic, anti-spasmodic, anodyne, sedative. Employed in tetanus, mania, epilepsy, chorea, palsy, and various nervous affections. Effectual in many acute pains, as in those arising from chronic diseases, or acute uterine affections, &c.

PREPARATIONS.

Fluid Extract.................................Dose, 5 to 20 Drops.
Solid Extract.................................. " 1-2 to 1 Grain.
Pills ....1-2 and 1 Grain each.

TINCTURE OF STRAMONIUM.

Fluid Extract...................................Two Ounces.
Diluted Alcohol.................................One Pint.

Dose—Half to one-and-a-half drams, and increase.

WINE OF STRAMONIUM.

Fluid Extract ....Two Ounces.
Sherry Wine.....................................Eight Ounces.
Alcohol...One Ounce.

Dose—Quarter to one dram.

PILLS OF STRAMONIUM.

Solid Extract...................................Half Grain.

Then bathe the part affected with the following mixture:

Fluid Extract of Capsicum.......................Half Dram.
Gum Camphor ....Ten Grains.
Crude Iodine....................................Ten Grains.
Diluted Alcohol.................................Two Ounces.

Remedy for Neuralgia.—Half an hour before the expected attack, give the pill, and bathe the part until warmth is produced. *Hunton.*

COMPOUND PILLS OF STRAMONIUM.

Solid Extract of Stramonium................Four Grains.
" " " Hyoscyamus................Fifteen Grains.
" " " Hop.......................One Dram.
Sulphate of Morphia.......................One-and-a-half Grains.

Mix, and divide into thirty pills.

In all forms of chronic diseases attended with acute pain, where opium is contra-indicated, this combination may be given with advantage.—*H. Green.*

COMPOUND PILLS OF STRAMONIUM.

Solid Extract of Stramonium... ....Ten Grains.
" " " Savin..........................Twenty-five Grains.
Powdered Camphor...........................One Dram.
" Seneka.............................Four Scruples.

Make into two grain pills. Dose—Four, three times a day. In rheumatism.

DIGITALIS PURPUREA.

Foxglove

Foxglove has a faint narcotic odour when dried, and a bitter, nauseous taste. It grows wild in the temperate parts of Europe, and in this country is cultivated both as an ornamental plant and for medicinal purposes. The leaves are the parts usually employed.

MEDICAL PROPERTIES.

Is narcotic, sedative and diuretic; sometimes emetic and purgative. It is prescribed as a sedative in hypertrophy of the heart and in aneurism of the large vessels proceeding from it; in inflammatory diseases; in dropsy, on account of its great diuretic power; in hemorrhage, as a sedative. It possesses great power over the circulation, and is peculiar in its operation. It is one of those remedies which should never be administered without an accurate knowledge of their medicinal properties.

PREPARATIONS.

Fluid Extract ....Dose, 5 to 10 Drops.
Digitalin ....
Pills of Digitalin.............................1-2 Grain each.
" " Ext. Digitalis.........................1-2 " "
" " " " and Squill.................. 2 " "

TINCTURE OF FOXGLOVE.

Fluid Extract...............................Two Ounces.
Diluted Alcohol.............................One Pint.

Dose—One-third to three-quarters of a dram, or forty-five to ninety drops.

INFUSION OF FOXGLOVE.

Fluid Extract...............................Two Drams.
Tincture of Cinnamon........................Two Ounces.
Water ....Fourteen Ounces.

Dose—Two-and-a-half to five drams.

SYRUP OF FOXGLOVE.

Fluid Extract....................................Two Ounces.

Syrup...Fourteen Ounces.

Dose—One-third to two-thirds of a dram.

MIXTURE OF TINCTURE OF FOXGLOVE.

Fluid Extract of Foxglove........................Seven Minims.

" " " Opium........................Three Minims.

Diluted Alcohol..................................One Dram.

Distilled Water..................................Two Ounces.

Dose—One-and-a-half drams, two or three times a day, in hæmatopsis and incipient phthisis. *Ellis.*

MIXTURE OF FOXGLOVE AND ACETATE OF POTASSA.

Fluid Extract of Foxglove........................Forty Minims.

" " " Opium........................Three Minims.

Acetate of Potassa...............................One Dram.

Alcohol..One Dram.

Water..Four Ounces.

Dose—One-and-a-half to three drams, three times a day.

DIOSCOREA VILLOSA.

Wild Yam.

This is a slender vine, twining over bushes and fences, in thickets and hedges; very common southward. The root is the officinal part.

MEDICAL PROPERTIES.

Anti-spasmodic. Successfully used in bilious colic. The *dioscorein* possesses the properties of the crude root, and is held to be as much a specific in bilious colic as quinia is in intermittent.

PREPARATION.

Dioscorein.......................................Dose, 1 to 6 Grains.

EPIGÆA REPENS.

Trailing Arbutus.

The Arbutus grows in sandy woods and rocky soils, generally preferring the sides of hills, with a northern exposure. Its flowers exhale a rich, spicy fragrance, appearing in early spring. The leaves are the parts in use.

MEDICAL PROPERTIES.

Diuretic and astringent. Is highly beneficial in gravel and all diseases of the urinary organs. It is prepared and administered in the same way with the uva ursi and buchu. It acts similarly, and has given relief in cases where these have failed.

PREPARATION.

Fluid Extract...Dose, 1 to 2 Drams.

INFUSION OF ARBUTUS.

Fluid Extract..............................One Ounce.
Water..One Pint.
Dose—Two to four ounces.

ERGOTA.

Ergot. The Diseased Seeds of Secale Cereale.

It is uncertain how far its peculiar medical properties may depend upon the morbid substance of the grain or on the fungous matter associated with it.

MEDICAL PROPERTIES.

The ergot operates with great energy upon the contractile property of the uterus. It has been given to promote the expulsion of the placenta, to restrain inordinate hemorrhages after delivery, and to hasten the discharge of the fœtus in protracted cases of abortion. It has been successful in pulmonary hemorrhage, after all the usual means had failed.

PREPARATIONS.

Fluid Extract...1-2 to 1 Dram.
Pills...1 Grain each.

TINCTURE OF ERGOT.

Fluid Extract..............................Four Ounces.
Diluted Alcohol..............................One Pint.
Dose—Two-and-a-half to five drams.

INFUSION OF ERGOT.

Fluid Extract..............................One Ounce.
Water..One Pint.
Dose—Two ounces, to be repeated every twenty minutes.

WINE OF ERGOT.

Fluid Extract.................................Five Ounces.
Sherry Wine...................................One Pint.

Dose—Two to four drams in cases of labor; for other purposes, one to two drams.

SYRUP OF ERGOT.

Fluid Extract.................................Two Ounces.
Syrup...Fourteen Ounces.

Dose—Half to one ounce.

MIXTURE OF ERGOT.

Fluid Extract of Ergot........................One Dram.
" " " Cubebs....................One Ounce.
Tincture of Cinnamon..........................Half Dram.

Dose—Twenty to forty drops in gonorrhea and gleet. *Ryan.*

EUONYMUS ATROPURPUREUS.

Wahoo.

A small shrub or bush, growing in woods and thickets, in many portions of the United States. The bark of the root, which has a bitter and somewhat unpleasant taste, is the officinal portion.

MEDICAL PROPERTIES.

Tonic, laxative, alterative, diuretic and expectorant; successfully used in intermittents, dyspepsia, torpid state of the liver, constipation, dropsy, and pulmonary affections.

PREPARATION.

Fluid Extract.................................Dose, 1 to 2 Drams.

TINCTURE OF WAHOO.

Fluid Extract.................................Four Ounces.
Diluted Alcohol...............................Twelve Ounces.

Dose—Half to one ounce.

SYRUP OF WAHOO.

Fluid Extract.................................Two Ounces.
Syrup...One Pint.

Dose—One to two ounces.

EUPATORIUM PERFOLIATUM.

Boneset.

Indigenous; abounding in most parts of the United States. The tops and leaves are the medicinal portions.

MEDICAL PROPERTIES.

Tonic, diaphoretic, and in large doses, emetic and aperient. Used in colds, fevers, catarrhs, remittent and intermittent fevers, typhoid-pneumonia, dropsy, dyspepsia, and general debility. The ***Eupurpurin***, from the ***E. Purpureum***, is a most powerful diuretic. Used with excellent effect in all chronic urinary disorders.

PREPARATIONS

Fluid Extract....................................Dose, 1 to 2 Drams.
Solid Extract .... " 5 to 20 Grains.
Eupatorin.............................. " 1 to 2 "
Eupurpurin.............................. " 3 to 4 "
Pills ....2 Grains each.

TINCTURE OF BONESET.

Fluid Extract..............................Four Ounces.
Diluted Alcohol..............................One Pint.
Dose—One to two ounces.

INFUSION OF BONESET.

Fluid Extract..................................Three Ounces.
Water..One Pint.
Dose—To be taken ad libitum.

COMPOUND INFUSION OF BONESET.

Fluid Extract of Boneset.......................Six Ounces.
" " " Cascarilla ....One Dram.
Water......................................Fifteen Ounces.
Dose—Two to three ounces.

SYRUP OF BONESET.

Fluid Extract..................................Four Ounces.
Syrup ....Ten Ounces.
Dose—Two to four drams.

Eupurpurin....................................Three Grains.
Geraniin....................................Two Grains.
Pulverized Nux Vomica....................................One-tenth Grain.

Divide into two powders. One may be given every four hours daily in renal affections.

Eupurpurin....................................Two Scruples.
Xanthoxylin....................................One Scruple.
Strychnia....................................One Grain.

Make twenty powders. Dose—One, three or four times a day in suppression of the urine, torpor or paralysis of the kidneys or bladder, rheumatism, hepatic torpor, &c.

GELSEMINUM SEMPERVIRENS.

Yellow Jessamine.

The Yellow Jessamine abounds throughout the Southern States, and is extensively cultivated as an ornamental vine. The root is the officinal part.

MEDICAL PROPERTIES.

It is an excellent febrifuge; has proved efficacious in nervous and bilious headache, colds, pneumonia, hemorrhage, chorea, though it is in fevers especially in which its efficacy has been mostly observed. It is said to subdue in from two to twenty hours the most formidable and complicated as well as the most simple fevers incident to our country and climate, quieting all nervous irritability and excitement, equalizing the circulation, promoting perspiration, rectifying the secretions, without causing nausea, vomiting or purging, and is adapted to any stage of the disease. May be used in all forms of neuralgia, nervous headache, toothache, lockjaw or tetanus.

PREPARATIONS.

Fluid Extract.................................Dose, 3 to 20 Drops.
Gelseminin................................. " 1-2 to 2 Grains.

TINCTURE OF YELLOW JESSAMINE.

Fluid Extract....................................Four Ounces.
Alcohol....................................One Pint.

Dose—Fifteen to sixty drops, and increase.

GENTIANA LUTEA.

Gentian.

This plant grows among the Appenines, the Alps, the Pyrenees, and in other mountainous regions of Europe. The root, the only part used in medicine, is imported to this country from Germany. It is of the highest antiquity, and is said to have derived its name from Gentius, King of Illyria.

MEDICAL PROPERTIES.

It is a valuable tonic, adapted to those cases requiring the use of pure or simple bitters. It excites the appetite, invigorates the powers of digestion, and may be used in all cases of disease dependent on pure debility of the digestive organs, or requiring a general tonic. It has proved useful in dyspepsia, gout, hysteria, scrofula, intermittent fever, diarrhea, and worms, but is rather applicable to the condition of the stomach and system generally, than to any specific disease.

PREPARATIONS.

Fluid Extract of Gentian.........................Dose, 1-2 to 1 Dram.
" " " " Compound................ " 1-2 to 1 Dram.
Solid Extract.................................... " 3 to 15 Grains.
Pills of Ext. Gentian ....2 Grains each.

TINCTURE OF GENTIAN.

Fluid Extract................................Four Ounces.
Diluted Alcohol................................One Pint.

Dose—Two-and-a-half to five drams.

TINCTURE OF RHUBARB AND GENTIAN.

Fluid Extract of Rhubarb.......................Two Ounces.
" " " Gentian.......................Half Ounce.
Diluted Alcohol................................Two Pints.

Dose—Half to two ounces.

SYRUP OF GENTIAN.

Fluid Extract................................Two Ounces.
Syrup...Fourteen Ounces.

Dose—Half to one ounce.

WINE OF GENTIAN.

Fluid Extract of Gentian........................Half Ounce.
" " " Cinchona........................One Ounce.
" " " Orange Peel....................Two Drams.
" " " Canella........................One Dram.
Proof Spirit....................................Four-and-a-half Oz.
Sherry Wine...................................Thirty-six Ounces.

A stomachic bitter. Dose—Half to one ounce.

PILLS OF GENTIAN AND IRON.

Solid Extract of Gentian........................Two Scruples.
Quevenne's Iron..............................One Scruple.

Divide into twenty pills. Dose—One, three times a day.

PILLS OF GENTIAN AND SULPHATE OF IRON.

Sulphate of Iron..........................One Dram.
Solid Extract of Gentian........................Sufficient.

Divide into thirty pills. One to be taken morning, noon and night. In dyspepsia, &c.

GENTIAN COMPOUND.

Compounded of Gentian, Orange Peel, Cloves, Canella, Red Saunders.

GERANIUM MACULATUM.

Cranesbill.

This is an indigenous plant, growing in all parts of the United States, in open woods, and flowering from April to June. The root is officinal.

MEDICAL PROPERTIES.

A powerful astringent. Used in chronic diarrhea, cholera infantum, hemorrhages, &c. Dr. Bigelow speaks of it as a powerful astringent. Very similar to kino and catechu, and a useful substitute for the more expensive articles. It forms an excellent local application as a gargle in sore throats and ulcerations of the mouth, and is adapted to the treatment of such discharges as continue from debility after the removal of their exciting causes. The absence of unpleasant taste, and all other offensive qualities, renders it peculiarly serviceable in the cases of infants, and of persons with very delicate stomachs.

Geraniin is a superior agent in the first and second stages of dysentery, diarrhea and cholera morbus. It forms an excellent application to bleeding wounds, and in epistaxis.

PREPARATIONS

Fluid Extract....... ....Dose, 1-2 to 1 Dram.
Solid Extract.................................. " 3 to 15 Grains.
Geraniin .... " 1 to 5 Grains.
Pills of Geraniin.................................1 Grain each.
" " Ext. Geranium..........................2 Grains each.

TINCTURE OF CRANESBILL.

Fluid Extract..................................Two Ounces.
Diluted Alcohol...............................One Pint.

Dose—Two-and-a-half to four drams.

INFUSION OF CRANESBILL.

Fluid Extract...............................One Ounce.
Water.................. ....One Pint.

Dose—One to two ounces.

COMPOUND INFUSION OF CRANESBILL.

Fluid Extract of Cranesbill..................Half Ounce.
" " " Black Cohosh...............Half "
" " " Golden Seal................Half "
" " " Witch Hazel...............Half "
Water..Two Pints.

This forms an efficacious astringent wash in aphthous and other diseases of the mouth and throat, when unaccompanied with inflammation; it is also useful as an injection in leucorrhea, prolapsus ani, and prolapsus uteri.

J. K.

SYRUP OF CRANESBILL.

Fluid Extract..................................Two Ounces.
Syrup... .... Fourteen Ounces.

Dose—Four drams.

Geraniin.....................................Ten Grains.
Dioscorein .... " "
Caulophyllin.......................... .... " "

Dose—Six grains to an adult every fifteen or twenty minutes, in diarrhea and cholera morbus, when much pain and flatulency are present.

GILLENIA TRIFOLIATA.

Indian Physic.

This is an indigenous plant, growing from Canada to Florida, east of the Alleghany mountains. The bark of the root is used in medicine.

MEDICAL PROPERTIES

It is used the same as Ipecac, to which refer.

PREPARATION.

Fluid Extract.....................................Dose, 4 to 12 Drops.

TINCTURE OF GILLENIA.

Fluid Extract.....................................Two Drams.
Diluted Alcohol.....................................Eight Drams.
Dose—Ten to twenty drops.

SYRUP OF GILLENIA.

Fluid Extract.....................................One Dram.
Syrup.....................................Seven Drams.
Dose—Quarter to half a dram.

GOSSYPIUM HERBACEUM.

Cotton.

A native of tropical America. The long staple, including the varieties of sea-island, black seed, grows best in the lower country, and the short or green seed, in the upper districts. The bark of the root is the active medicinal part.

MEDICAL PROPERTIES.

Emmenagogue, parturient and abortive. It acts with as much efficiency and more safety than ergot. It operates without pain or gastric disturbance, producing no other effect than the excitation of the menstrual secretions, except perhaps some degree of anodyne influence. It is an excellent remedy in the treatment of chlorotic and anæmic females.

PREPARATION.

Fluid Extract.....................................Dose, 4 Drams.

INFUSION OF COTTON.

Fluid Extract............................Four Ounces.
Water...One Pint.

Dose—Two-and-a-half to five ounces.

HÆMATOXYLON CAMPECHIANUM.

Logwood.

This tree, occasionally reaching forty or fifty feet in height, is a native of tropical America, and has become naturalized in many of the West India islands. The dingy, cherry-red inner wood is the part used in medicine and the arts.

MEDICAL PROPERTIES.

It is tonic and astringent, without any irritating properties. May be used with much advantage in diarrhea, dysentery and in the relaxed condition of the bowels succeeding cholera-infantum. In constitutions broken down by disease, dissipation, or the excessive use of mercury, the decoction of logwood, used freely in connection with other treatment, will be found highly beneficial.

PREPARATIONS.

Fluid Extract...................................Dose, 1-2 to 1 Dram.
Solid Extract................................... " 5 to 30 Grains.
Pills..2 Grains each.

INFUSION OF LOGWOOD.

Fluid Extract...............................Half Ounce.
Water...One Pint.

Dose—Four drams every three or four hours in cholera and diarrhea.

Ellis.

MIXTURE OF LOGWOOD.

Fluid Extract...............................Three Drams.
Tincture of Catechu.......................Two Drams.
Water...Seven Ounces.

Dose—Half ounce, once in two or three hours, in the advanced stage of diarrhea and dysentery.

COMPOUND WINE OF LOGWOOD.

Fluid Extract of Logwood...................Four Ounces.
" " " Black Hellebore..............Four Ounces.
Sherry Wine..................................Three Pints.

Dose—Half to two ounces, three times a day. Cathartic, tonic and emmenagogue: useful in chlorosis, amenorrhea, and some forms of dysmenorrhea.

HAMAMELIS VIRGINICA.

Witch Hazel.

Named from its having fruit and flowers together on the same tree. It grows in most parts of the United States. The bark and leaves are the parts used in medicine.

MEDICAL PROPERTIES.

Witch Hazel is tonic, astringent and sedative; used in hemoptysis, hematemesis, and other hemorrhages, as well as in diarrhea, dysentery, and excessive mucous discharges; in incipient phthisis in which it is supposed to possess an anodyne influence, also for sore mouth, painful tumors.

PREPARATION.

Fluid Extract....................................Dose, 1 to 2 Drams.

INFUSION OF WITCH HAZEL.

Fluid Extract.................................One Ounce.
Water...One Pint.

Dose—Four drams every five minutes in cases of epistaxis.

SYRUP OF WITCH HAZEL.

Fluid Extract.................................Four Ounces.
Syrup...Twelve Ounces.

Dose—One to two drams.

WASH IN TINEA CAPITIS.

Fluid Extract of Witch Hazel...................One Ounce.
" " " Myrica Cerifera...............One Ounce.
Sesqui-carbonate of Potassa....................Fifteen Grains.
Water..Eight Ounces.

Wash the affected parts twice a day with a solution of castile soap, and after thoroughly drying them, apply the above lotion. *D. E. Smith.*

HELLEBORUS NIGER.

Black Hellebore.

A native of the mountainous regions of southern and temperate Europe, entirely distinct from the Hellebore of the ancients. The fibres of the roots are the portions usually recommended for medicinal use.

MEDICAL PROPERTIES.

It is a drastic hydragogue cathartic, possessed of emmenagogue powers; occasionally found useful in chlorosis, amenorrhea, &c.

PREPARATIONS.

Fluid Extract.................................Dose, 10 to 20 Drops.
Solid Extract................................. " 1 to 5 Grains.
Pills...1 Grain each.

TINCTURE OF BLACK HELLEBORE.

Fluid Extract..............................Two Ounces.
Diluted Alcohol............................One Pint.

Dose—Thirty drops to one dram.

COMPOUND TINCTURE OF BLACK HELLEBORE.

Tincture of Black Hellebore..................Half Ounce.
" " Myrrh..........................One Ounce.
" " Spanish Flies....................Two Drams.

Dose—Thirty drops three times a day as an emmenagogue.

COMPOUND WINE OF BLACK HELLEBORE.

Fluid Extract of Black Hellebore.............One Ounce.
" " " Wormwood.................Two Ounces.
White Wine...............................Four Pints.

Dose—Half to one dram. *Brunner.*

COMPOUND PILLS OF BLACK HELLEBORE.

Solid Extract of Black Hellebore..............Five Grains.
Calomel...................................... " "
Powdered Ipecac..........................Three "
Syrup of Ginger............................Sufficient.

Mix, and make four pills. Two to be taken every four hours till a full purgation is caused. *Ainslie.*

OINTMENT OF BLACK HELLEBORE.

Solid Extract of Black Hellebore...............One Dram.
Lard......................................One Ounce.

Application for obstinate herpetic eruptions. *Soubieran.*

HELONIAS DIOICA.

False Unicorn.

This plant is indigenous to the United States, abundant in some of the Western States, growing in woodlands, meadows, and moist situations. The root is the part used in medicine.

MEDICAL PROPERTIES.

Tonic, diuretic and vermifuge. Beneficial in colic and in atony of the generative organs. It acts as a uterine tonic in leucorrhea, amenorrhea, and to remove the tendency to repeated and successive miscarriages.

PREPARATIONS.

Fluid Extract....................................Dose, 1 to 3 Drams.
Helonin.. " 1-2 to 1 Grain.

HEPATICA AMERICANA.

Liverwort.

An indigenous plant, growing in woods, upon the sides of hills and mountains. The leaves resist the cold of winter, and the flowers appear early in the spring. The whole plant is used.

MEDICAL PROPERTIES.

Liverwort is a very mild, demulcent tonic and astringent, supposed by some to possess diuretic and deobstruent virtues. It has been used in fevers, hepatic complaints, hemoptysis, coughs, &c.

PREPARATION.

Fluid Extract....................................Dose, 2 to 3 Drams.

INFUSION OF LIVERWORT.

Fluid Extract....................................Four Ounces.
Water....................................One Pint.

To be taken *ad libitum*.

SYRUP OF LIVERWORT.

Fluid Extract....................................Three Ounces.
Syrup....................................Six Ounces.

Dose—Two to three ounces.

HUMULUS LUPULUS.

Hop.

The Hop is a native of North America and Europe. The part of the plant used, as well in the preparation of malt liquors as in medicine, is the fruit or strobiles.

MEDICAL PROPERTIES.

Hops are tonic and moderately narcotic, and have been recommended in diseases of local and general debility, associated with morbid vigilance, or other nervous derangement. Useful in dyspepsia and the nervous tremors, wakefulness, and delirium of drunkard. The Lupulin is a powerful antaphrodisiac, composer of the genital organs, and quieter of painful erections. In a large number of cases of painful erections, dependent upon gonorrhea, lupulin quieted the erethisms in four-fifths.

PREPARATIONS.

Fluid Extract.................................Dose, 1-2 to 1 Dram.
Solid Extract.................................. " 5 to 20 Grains.
Lupulin.. " 6 to 10 Grains.

TINCTURE OF HOPS.

Fluid Extract.................................Five Ounces.
Diluted Alcohol...............................Two Pints.
Dose—Three to six drams.

INFUSION OF HOPS.

Fluid Extract.................................Four Drams.
Water...One Pint.
Dose—Two to four ounces.

MIXTURE OF HOPS.

Fluid Extract of Hops.................... x-and-a-half Drams.
" " " Orange Peel.......................One Dram.
Syrup...Eight Drams.
Alcohol.......................................Eight Drams.
Water...Seven Ounces.
Dose—Four drams.

TINCTURE OF LUPULIN.

Lupulin.......................................Four Ounces.
Alcohol.......................................Two Pints.

Macerate for fourteen days, and filter through paper. Dose—One to two drams, in mucilage or sweetened water.

Fifteen to thirty grains of Lupulin, triturated with white sugar, has been found extremely efficacious in priapism, chordee, and spermatorrhea, acting as an anaphrodisiac. *M. Debout.*

HYDRANGEA ARBORESCENS.

Hydrangea.

The Hydrangea grows abundantly in the Southern, Middle and Western States. The root is the officinal part.

MEDICAL PROPERTIES

This plant was introduced to the medical profession by Dr. S. W. Butler, of Burlington, N. J., as a remedy for the removal of calculus or stony deposits in the bladder, and for relieving the excruciating pain attendant on the passage of a calculus through the urethra. The power of curing stone in the bladder is not claimed for it; it is only while the deposits are small, when in that form of the disease known as gravel, that it is an efficient remedy; then by removing the nucleus, which if allowed to remain in the organ would increase in size and form stone, the disease is averted. Employed at this stage it is said to have proved beneficial in every instance; and as many as one hundred and twenty calculi have been known to come from one person under the use of this remedy. The effect, says Dr. Butler, is to remove, by its own specific action on the bladder, such deposits as may be contained in that viscus, provided they are small enough to pass through the urethra.

PREPARATION.

Fluid Extract.................................Dose, 1 to 2 Drams.

HYDRASTIS CANADENSIS.

Golden Seal.

The Hydrastis is found in different parts of the United States and Canadas, though it is most abundant west of the Alleghanies. The root is the officinal part.

MEDICAL PROPERTIES.

Used in dyspepsia, chronic affections of the nervous coats of the stomach, erysipelas, remittent, intermittent and typhoid fevers, torpor of the liver, and where tonics are required. In combination with Geranium it forms an efficient remedy in chronic diarrhea and dysentery.

The Hydrastin is a tonic, with an especial action on diseased mucous tissues, and particularly beneficial during convalescence from exhausting diseases.

PREPARATIONS.

Fluid Extract ....Dose, 1-2 to 2 Drams.
Solid Extract.................................. " 2 to 5 Grains.
Hydrastin (Resinoid).......................... " 1-2 to 5 "
Hydrastin (Neutral)........................... " 2 to 6 "
Hydrastina (Alkaloid)......................... " 1 to 5 "
Pills of Hydrastin (Neutral).....................1 Grain each.
" " Hydrastina..............................1 " "

TINCTURE OF GOLDEN SEAL.

Fluid Extract..................................Three Ounces.
Diluted Alcohol................................One Pint.

Dose—Half to one-and-a-half ounces.

COMPOUND TINCTURE OF GOLDEN SEAL

Fluid Extract of Golden Seal.....................Two Ounces.
" " " Lobelia.........................Two Ounces.
Diluted Alcohol................................One Pint.

Dose—One to two-and-a-half drams.

LOTION OF GOLDEN SEAL AND ACONITE.

Fluid Extract of Golden Seal.....................Four Drams.
" " " Aconite.........................Half Dram.
Water.......................................Four Ounces.

COMPOUND INFUSION OF GOLDEN SEAL.

Fluid Extract of Golden Seal..... ....Half Ounce.
" " " Blue Cohosh.................... " "
" " " Witch Hazel.................... " "
Pulverized Alum.................................One Dram.
Honey ....Three Drams.
Water..One Pint.

Valuable as a wash or gargle in various forms of sore mouth and ulcerated sore throat.

Hydrastin ....Four Grains.
Myricin.................................. " "
Xanthoxylin.............................. " "

Make into two-grain powders. Efficacious in jaundice.

Hydrastin ....Six Grains.
Caulophyllin............................. " "
Leptandrin............................... " "

Make into three-grain powders. Excellent in apthæ and ulcerations of the mouth and throat, especially in adults.

Hydrastin.................................Twenty Grains.
Leptandrin................................Ten "
Podophyllin ....Two-and-a-half Grains.
Sugar of Milk.............................One Dram.

Mix well, and divide into twenty powders. One to be given every two hours. Acts not only as an efficient hepatic stimulant, but also as a tonic to the enfeebled mucous membrane in epidemic dysentery. *Pretbyman.*

HYOSCYAMUS NIGER.

Henbane.

Rare in this country, but grows abundantly in Great Britain and the continent of Europe. All the parts are active. The U. S. Pharmacopeia recognizes the seeds and leaves. The root is said to be much more poisonous in the second year than in the first.

MEDICAL PROPERTIES.

It ranks among the narcotics. It accelerates the circulation, increases the general warmth, occasions a sense of heat in the throat, and after a short period induces sleep. It does not constipate like opium, but often proves laxative. It is most frequently applied in neuralgic and spasmodic affections, rheumatism, gout, hysteria and various pectoral diseases, such as catarrh, pertussis, asthma, phthisis, &c.

PREPARATIONS.

Fluid Extract.............................Dose, 10 to 20 Drops.
Solid Extract............................. " 1-2 to 1 Grain.
Hyoscyamin................................ " 1-8 to 1-2 "
Pills of Ext. Hyoscyamus..................1-4, 1-2 and 1 Grain each.

TINCTURE OF HYOSCYAMUS.

Fluid Extract................................Four Ounces.
Diluted Alcohol..............................Two Pints.

Dose—Half to one-and-a-half drams.

INFUSION OF HYOSCYAMUS.

Fluid Extract................................Half Ounce.
Water..One Pint.

As a lotion. *Ellis.*

COMPOUND PILLS OF HYOSCYAMUS.

Solid Extract of Hyoscyamus..................Two Drams.
" " " Valerian.............................. " "
" " " Aconite...............................One "
Sulphate of Quinia .... " "

Mix, and divide into thre -grain pills. Dose—One pill every two or three hours. Very advantageous in neuralgia, rheumatism, chorea, dysmenorrhea and affections of a similar character.

PILLS OF HENBANE, OPIUM, AND CONIUM.

Solid Extract of Hyoscyamus..................Ten Grains.
" " " Opium.................................Four "
" " " Conium................................Fifteen "

Make twenty pills. One to be taken every night when an anodyne is required.

PILLS OF HENBANE AND IPECAC.

Solid Extract of Hyoscyamus..................Ten Grains.
Powdered Ipecac..............................Five Grains.

Make into ten pills. Dose—One, every hour, or until relief is procured, watching the effect. In flatulence and irritability of the bowels.

PILLS OF HENBANE AND IRON.

Solid Extract of Hyoscyamus..............One-and-a-half Scruples.
Valerianate of Iron..........................One Dram.

Mix, and divide into twenty pills. Dose—One, three times a day.

Of advantage in all the neuralgic affections of anæmic and debilitated females. *H. Green.*

IPOMÆA JALAPA.

Jalap.

The Jalap plant is a native of Mexico, and derives its name from Xalapa, in the neighborhood of which it grows, 6000 feet above the level of the ocean. The tuber is the part used in medicine.

MEDICAL PROPERTIES.

It is an active cathartic, operating briskly, and sometimes painfully upon the bowels, producing copious and watery stools. It is advantageously employed in dropsy, in the treatment of hip disease, and scrofulous affections of the other joints.

PREPARATIONS.

Fluid Extract..........Dose, 1-4 to 1 Dram.
Solid Extract .... " 3 to 8 Grains.
Jalapin .... " 1 to 2 Grains.
Pills of Ext. Jalap..........1 Grain each.
Pills of Jalapin..........1 " "

TINCTURE OF JALAP.

Fluid Extract..........Six Ounces.
Diluted Alcohol..........Three Pints.

Dose—One to two-and-a-half drams.

COMPOUND PILLS OF JALAP.

Solid Extract of Jalap..........Half Ounce.
Bitartrate of Potash..........One Ounce.

Make into fifty pills. A hydrogogue purgative, useful in costiveness, worms, and several forms of dropsy.

MIXTURE OF JALAP AND CREAM OF TARTAR.

Solid Extract of Jalap..........One Dram.
Cream of Tartar..........Six Drams.

Make into thirty pills. Dose, three every three hours, as a hydrogogue purgative.

GRIFFITH'S CATHARTIC PILLS.

Solid Extract of Jalap..........Seven Grains.
" " " Rhubarb..........Six Grains.

Soap...Half Dram.
Mild Chloride of Mercury.....................Twenty-five Grains.
Tartrate of Antimony and Potassa...........One-and-a-half Grains.
Distilled Water...............................Sufficient.

Divide into twenty-five pills, two of which may be taken at once, and repeated in two hours, if necessary.

IRIS FLORENTINA.

Orris.

A native of the southern parts of Europe.

MEDICAL PROPERTIES.

Possesses cathartic properties, and, in large doses, acts as an emetic Chiefly used in compounds, on account of the agreeable odor it imparts.

PREPARATION.

Fluid Extract—To be used in compounds, at discretion.

IRIS VERSICOLOR.

Blue Flag.

The Blue Flag is found in most parts of the United States, flourishing in low, wet places, bearing large and beautiful flowers. The root is the medicinal portion.

MEDICAL PROPERTIES.

A potent remedy in dropsy, scrofula, hepatic, renal and splenitic affections. It acts more particularly on the glandular system, and in large doses it evacuates and exhausts the system, acting on the liver, and the alimentary canal throughout, fulfilling most of the indications of mercury. The *Iridin* is extensively used in chronic visceral affections, diseases of the genital organs, rheumatism and dropsy, being also an effective sialogogue in those cases of glandular diseases which seem to resist the action of other means.

PREPARATIONS.

Fluid Extract..................................Dose, 20 to 60 Drops.
Solid Extract.................................. " 1 to 4 Grains.
Iridin... " 1-2 to 5 Grains.
Pills of Ext. Iris Versicol........................1 Grain each.
" " Iridin.......................................1-2 and 1 Grain each.

TINCTURE OF BLUE FLAG.

Fluid Extract................................Two Ounces.
Diluted Alcohol................................One Pint.
Dose—One to three drams.

SYRUP OF BLUE FLAG.

Fluid Extract................................Two Ounces.
Syrup... ....Fourteen Ounces.
Dose—One-and-a-half to four drams.

COMPOUND TINCTURE OF BLUE FLAG.

Fluid Extract of Blue Flag............... ....One Dram.
" " " Mandrake.....................Half Dram.
Powdered Nux Vomica........................Two Drams.
Diluted Alcohol ....Ten-and-a-half Drams.
Dose—Ten to twenty drops in water, two or three times a day.

Iridin......................................Three Grains.
Leptandrin..................................Six "
Bitartrate of Potassa .. ..Twenty "
This forms an excellent hydragogue cathartic powder of much value in some forms of dropsy.

Iridin......................................Three Grains.
Podophyllin .. .. " "
Xanthoxylin .... " "
To be given in grain doses every hour or two. A valuable sialogogue.

JUGLANS CINEREA.

Butternut.

The Butternut grows in Upper and Lower Canada, and throughout the whole northern, eastern and western sections of the United States.

MEDICAL PROPERTIES.

A mild cathartic. Very efficacious in habitual constipation, dysentery, and other affections of the bowels. It evacuates without debilitating the alimentary canal. It is much employed as a domestic remedy in intermittent and remittent fevers, as well as in other diseases attended with congestion of the abdominal viscera. The *juglandin* answers an admirable purpose as a laxative and cathartic.

PREPARATIONS.

Fluid Extract ....Dose, 1 to 2 Drams.
Solid Extract.. " 5 to 20 Grains.
Juglandin... " 1 to 5 Grains.

PILLS OF BUTTERNUT AND JALAP.

Solid Fxtract of Butternut................One-and-a-quarter Drams.
" " " Jalap......................Three-quarters Dram.
Soap..Ten Grains.

Mix, and divide into fifteen pills. Three or four at a dose, and more if these do not operate. *Ellis.*

JUNIPERUS SABINA.

Savin.

The tops of the plant are officinal. It is a native of the Levant and south of Europe, and is said to grow wild in the neighborhood of our N. W. Lakes.

MEDICAL PROPERTIES.

It is highly stimulant, increasing most of the secretions, especially those of the skin and uterus, to the latter of which organs it seems to have a peculiar direction; though in cases of pregnancy must be used with caution. Useful in complaints of the kidney, suppression of urine and suppressed menstruation.

PREPARATIONS.

Fluid Extract.................. ....Dose, 10 to 30 Drops.
Solid Extract.. " 1 to 5 Grains.
Pills...1 Grain each.

TINCTURE OF SAVIN.

Fluid Extract...................................Four Ounces.
Diluted Alcohol...............................One Pint.

Dose—Half to one-and-a-half drams.

INFUSION OF SAVIN.

Fluid Extract...................................Two Drams.
Water ....Eight Ounces.

Dose—Half to one ounce.

COMPOUND TINCTURE OF SAVIN.

Fluid Extract of Savin........................Four Ounces.
" " " Ergot........................One Ounce.
" " " Water Pepper..................One Ounce.
" " " Blue Cohosh....................Two Ounces.
Diluted Alcohol..............................Twelve Ounces.

Dose—One dram, three or four times a day.

MIXTURE OF SAVIN AND GINGER.

Fluid Extract of Savin........................Half Dram.
" " " Ginger........................One Dram.
Sulphate of Potassa..... ....Two Drams.

Dose—Half dram, twice a day in amenorrhea. *Ellis.*

KRAMERIA TRIANDRA.

Rhatany.

This species is a native of Peru, usually growing on the sides of mountains, and flowering throughout the year. It was long known to the natives as a powerful astringent, previous to its discovery in 1780 by Ruiz.

MEDICAL PROPERTIES.

It is a powerful astringent, with tonic properties. Used internally with advantage in menorrhagia, hematemesis, passive hemorrhages, chronic diarrhea, leucorrhea, chronic mucous discharges and incontinence of urine; also as a local application in prolapsus ani, fissure of the anus and leucorrhea.

PREPARATIONS.

Fluid Extract..................................Dose, 1-2 to 1 Dram.
Solid Extract.................................. " 5 to 20 Grains.
Pills ....1 Grain each.

TINCTURE OF RHATANY.

Fluid Extract..................................Six Ounces.
Diluted Alcohol..............................Two Pints.

Dose—Three to six drams.

INFUSION OF RHATANY.

Fluid Extract..................................Two Ounces.
Water...One Pint.

Dose—Half to one ounce.

SYRUP OF RHATANY.

Fluid Extract....................................Four Ounces.
Syrup ....Twelve Ounces.

Dose—Two to four drams.

MIXTURE OF RHATANY AND POPPY.

Fluid Extract of Rhatany........................One Dram.
" " " Poppy...........................Two Drams.
Rose Water ....Two Ounces.
Syrup..Two Ounces.

Dose—One to two drams, in passive hemorrhages and chronic dysentery.

Fouquier.

LACTUCA SATIVA.

Lettuce.

The milky juice of the garden lettuce possesses medicinal, as well as sensible properties. This juice is more abundant in the wild than in the cultivated plants.

MEDICAL PROPERTIES.

Is usually given to quiet nervous irritability and allay cough. It may be given when opium is indicated, but cannot be given from idiosyncracy of the patient. It does not produce that disturbance of the functions which usually follows opium.

PREPARATIONS.

Fluid Extract....................................Dose, 1-2 to 2 Drams.
Solid Extract.................................... " 2 to 5 Grains.
Pills..2 Grains each.

SYRUP OF LETTUCE.

Fluid Extract....................................Two Ounces.
Syrup..Fourteen Ounces.

Dose—Half to two ounces.

COMPOUND SYRUP OF POPPY AND LETTUCE.

Fluid Extract of Lettuce........................Two Ounces.
" " " Poppy...........................Four Ounces.
Syrup..Ten Ounces.

Dose—Half to one dram.

MIXTURE OF LETTUCE AND FOXGLOVE.

Fluid Extract of Lettuce........................Four Drams.
" " " Foxglove......................Thirty-two Drops.
Cinnamon Water................................One Dram.
Dose—Thirty to fifty drops.

LAPPA MINOR.

Burdock.

Native of Europe, and abundant in the United States. The root is used in medicine.

MEDICAL PROPERTIES.

Useful in scorbutic, syphilitic, scrofulous, gouty, leprous and nephritic diseases. To prove effectual, its use must be persevered in for a long time. As an ointment, it has been employed with advantage in cutaneous diseases and obstinate ulcers.

PREPARATIONS.

Fluid Extract..................................Dose, 1 Dram.
Solid Extract...... ...." 5 to 20 Grains.
Pills..2 Grains each.

TINCTURE OF BURDOCK.

Fluid Extract.................................Two Ounces.
Diluted Alcohol...............................One Pint.
Dose—One ounce.

INFUSION OF BURDOCK.

Fluid Extract.................................One Ounce.
Water...One Pint.
Dose—Two to four ounces.

SYRUP OF BURDOCK.

Fluid Extract ....Four Ounces.
Syrup...Twelve Ounces.
Dose—Half to one ounce.

COMPOUND SYRUP OF BURDOCK.

Fluid Extract of Burdock......................One Ounce.
" " " Yellow Dock.................. " "
" " " Dandelion.................... " "

Fluid Extract of Sarsaparilla....................One Ounce.
" " " Sassafras.......................To flavor.

Syrup ....Two Pints.
Dose—Half to one-and-a-half ounces.

LAURUS SASSAFRAS.

Sassafras.

The Sassafras is common throughout the United States. The root is directed by the British Pharmacopeias; the bark of the root and the pith of the twigs and extreme branches, by that of the U. S.

MEDICAL PROPERTIES.

Stimulant, and perhaps diaphoretic. It is used mainly as an adjuvant to other medicines, the flavor of which it improves. It has been particularly recommended in chronic rheumatism, cutaneous eruptions, scorbutic and syphiloid affections.

PREPARATION.

Fluid Extract....................................Dose, 1 to 2 Drams.

TINCTURE OF SASSAFRAS.

Fluid Extract...............................Three Ounces.
Diluted Alcohol ....Seven Ounces.
Dose—One ounce.

INFUSION OF SASSAFRAS.

Fluid Extract................................Two Ounces.
Water...One Pint.
Drink *ad libitum.*

LEONTICE THALICTROIDES.

Blue Cohosh.

A perennial plant, growing all over the United States, in low, moist, rich grounds. The officinal part is the root.

MEDICAL PROPERTIES.

Possessed of diuretic, diaphoretic and anthelmintic properties; is a valuable agent in all chronic uterine diseases; appears to exert an especial influence upon the uterus; has been successfully employed in rheumatism, dropsy, colic, hiccough, epilepsy, uterine leucorrhea, amenorrhea, &c. In decoction, blue cohosh is preferable to ergot in expediting delivery, in all those cases where the delay is owing to debility, or want of uterine nervous energy, or is the result of fatigue.

PREPARATIONS.

Fluid Extract....................................Dose, 15 to 40 Drops.
Solid Extract.................................... " 1 to 5 Grains.
Caulophyllin................... .... " 1-4 to 4 Grains.
Pills....................................2 Grains each.

TINCTURE OF BLUE COHOSH.

Fluid Extract....................................Three Ounces.
Diluted Alcohol....................................One Pint.

Dose—Half to one dram.

INFUSION OF BLUE COHOSH.

Fluid Extract....................................One Ounce.
Water ....One Pint.

Dose—Two to four ounces.

SYRUP OF BLUE COHOSH.

Fluid Extract....................................Two Ounces.
Syrup....................................Fourteen Ounces.

Dose—One to one-and-a-half drams.

GARGLE OF BLUE COHOSH.

Fluid Extract of Blue Cohosh...................One Ounce.
" " " Golden Seal...................One "
Water....................................Eight Ounces.

An effectual wash for apthous sore mouth and throat.

MIXTURE OF BLUE COHOSH.

Fluid Extract of Blue Cohosh...................Two Ounces.
" " " Ergot...................One Ounce.
" " " Water Pepper...................One Ounce.
" " " Savin...................Two Ounces.

Dose—Twenty to forty drops, two or three times a day. An emmenagogue tincture, useful in amenorrhea, dysmenorrhea, and other uterine affections.

Caulophyllin ....Twelve Grains.
Cimicifugin ....Twelve "
Carbonate of Ammonia ....Twelve "

Dose—Six grains. Valuable in the unhealthy condition of the uterus and appendages, and as an anti-spasmodic in epilepsy, rheumatism, hysteria, and dropsy.

Caulophyllin ....Ten Grains.
Dioscorein ....Eight Grains.

Dose—Three to six grains, in bilious colic and flatulence.

Caulophyllin ....Twelve Grains.
Podophyllin ....Ten "
Muriate of Ammonia ....Ten "

Dose—Three to five grains. Excellent in nephritic diseases, accompanied with pains of a spasmodic character.

LEONURUS CARDIACA.

Motherwort.

Supposed to be a native of Tartary. The whole plant is officinal.

MEDICAL PROPERTIES.

Recommended in nervous complaints, in irritable habits, delirium tremens, in all chronic diseases attended with restlessness, wakefulness, disturbed sleep, spinal irritation, neuralgic pains, and in liver affections.

PREPARATIONS.

Solid Extract ....Dose, 3 to 6 Grains.
Pills ....2 Grains each.

COMPOUND PILLS OF MOTHERWORT.

Solid Extract of Motherwort ....Two Drams.
" " " Unicorn Root ....Two Drams.
Leptandrin ....One Dram.
Cimicifugin ....One Dram.

Mix, and divide into sixty pills.

Dose—One, every one, two or three hours, according to the case. These pills act as a uterine tonic and alterative. *J. K.*

LEPTANDRA VIRGINICA.

Culver's Root.

This plant grows throughout the United States, in limestone countries, and flowers in July and August. The root is the officinal part.

MEDICAL PROPERTIES.

Tonic, cholagogue and laxative; is employed in hepatic affections, as it acts upon the liver with energy and without active catharsis; in bilious and typhoid fevers as a laxative and tonic, and in dyspepsia, diarrhea and dysentery.

The *Leptandrin* may be safely and efficaciously employed in the treatment of diarrhea, cholera infantum, some forms of dyspepsia, typhoid fever, and all diseases connected with biliary derangements.

PREPARATIONS.

Fluid Extract ....Dose, 1-3 to 1 Dram.
Leptandrin...................... " 1-4 to 1 Grain in acute cases.
" .... " 1 to 2 Grains in chronic cases.
Pills of Leptandrin....................1 Grain each.

TINCTURE OF LEPTANDRA.

Fluid Extract................................Two Ounces.
Diluted Alcohol................................One Pint.

Dose—Half to one ounce.

SYRUP OF LEPTANDRA.

Fluid Extract................................Four Ounces.
Syrup... ....Eight Ounces.

Dose—One-and-a-half to three drams.

COMPOUND PILLS OF LEPTANDRIN.

Leptandrin .. ..One Dram.
Podophyllin...... ....Half Dram.
Solid Ext. Rhubarb........... ....Sufficient.

Mix, and divide into sixty pills Dose—One to two pills once or twice a day. Valuable hydragogue. Beneficial in liver affections, obstinate constipation, or whenever catharsis is required.

MIXTURE OF LEPTANDRIN

Leptandrin .... Six Grains.
Quinia .... Three Grains.
Camphor .... One-and-a-half Grains.
Powdered Ipecac .... Three-quarters Grain.

Divide into twelve powders. One may be given every two or three hours, and used for several days. Excellent in cholera infantum.

Charcoal .... One Dram.
Leptandrin .... Three Grains.

Make twelve powders. Dose—One every two or three hours.

LIATRIS SPICATA

Button Snakeroot.

This and the *L. Squarrosa* and *L. Scariosa* are splendid native plants. The roots are the officinal parts.

MEDICAL PROPERTIES.

Diuretic, tonic, stimulant and emmenagogue. The infusion is efficacious in gleet, gonorrhea and nephritic diseases; also in scrofula, dysmenorrhea, amenorrhea, after-pains, &c. Of advantage also as a gargle in sore throat.

PREPARATIONS.

Fluid Extract .... Dose, 1 to 2 Drams
Liatrin .... " 4 to 8 Grains

INFUSION OF LIATRIS.

Fluid Extract .... Two Ounces.
Water .... One Pint.

Dose—Two to four ounces.

MIXTURE OF LIATRIS.

Fluid Extract of Liatris .... One Ounce
" " " Lycopus Virginicus .... " "
" " " Aletris Farinosa .... " "

Dose—One to three drams.
Beneficial in Bright's disease.

LOBELIA INFLATA.

Lobelia.

The Lobelia is a common weed, growing on the road sides and in neglected fields throughout the United States. The plant was named in honor of Matthias de Lobel, physician and botanist to James I. All its parts are officinal, though the root and inflated capsules are most powerful.

MEDICAL PROPERTIES.

Lobelia is emetic, and in small doses, diaphoretic and expectorant. It is of especial advantage in spasmodic asthma, and is used in catarrh, croup, pertussis, and other laryngeal and pectoral affections. In cases where relaxation is required, either to subdue spasm or otherwise, lobelia will be found to be a valuable article.

PREPARATIONS.

Fluid Extract of Lobelia.............	Dose—	Expectorant, 10 to 60 Drops.
" " " "	"	Emetic, 1-4 to 1 Dram.
" " " " Compound....	"	10 to 60 Drops, and 1-4 to 1 Dram.
Lobelin..........................	"	1-2 to 1 1-2 Grains.

TINCTURE OF LOBELIA.

Fluid Extract.................................Two Ounces.
Diluted Alcohol..............................One Pint.

Dose—As an anti-spasmodic, one to three drams: as an emetic, half ounce.

INFUSION OF LOBELIA

Fluid Extract.................................One Ounce.
Water...One Pint.

Dose—An ounce every half hour till vomiting ensues. *Ellis.*

SYRUP OF LOBELIA.

Fluid Extract.................................Two Ounces.
Syrup...Ten Ounces.

Dose—Two drams. *W. Procter.*

VINEGAR OF LOBELIA.

Fluid Extract.................................Four Ounces.
Diluted Acetic Acid...........................Twenty Ounces.

Dose—Two drams. *W. Procter.*

7

MIXTURE FOR CHRONIC COUGH.

Fluid Extract of Squill........................Half Dram.
" " " Lobelia........................Half "
" " " Opium........................Half "
Syrup..Two Ounces.
Diluted Alcohol..............................One-and-a-half Oz.
Dose—Half dram.

LOBELIA MIXTURE.

Tincture of Lobelia..........................Half Ounce.
" " Bloodroot........................Two Ounces.
Oil of Spearmint.............................Half Dram.
Empyreumatic Syrup...........................Five Ounces.
Dose—Half dram every two hours.

Of magical efficacy in all cases where an expectorant and sudorific are indicated; in catarrhal affections, spasmodic croup, pertussis, asthma, and in subduing mucous inflammation about the throat and air passages.

Boston Med. Journal.

LOBELIA COMPOUND.

Compounded of Lobelia, Bloodroot, Skunk Cabbage.

LYCOPUS VIRGINICUS.

Bugle-weed.

This plant grows in shady and wet places throughout the greater part of the United States. The whole herb is used.

MEDICAL PROPERTIES.

A mild narcotic, sedative, sub-astringent, styptic. A valuable remedy for hemorrhage from the lungs, incipient phthisis, pneumonia; useful in quieting irritation and allaying cough; it appears to act like digitalis in abating the frequency of the pulse, but is far less active; allays nervous and internal excitement, and is useful for internal hemorrhages. A slight tonic, and taken warm, a good diaphoretic.

PREPARATION.

Fluid Extract..................................Dose, 1 to 2 Drams.

INFUSION OF BUGLE.

Fluid Extract..................................One Ounce
Water..One Pint.
Dose—Two to four ounces.

SYRUP OF BUGLE.

Fluid Extract.................................Three Ounces.
Syrup...Twelve Ounces.
Dose—One to two ounces.

MARRUBIUM VULGARE.

Horehound.

The plant has been naturalized in this country from Europe; has a strong, agreeable odor, which is diminished by drying, and is lost by keeping. The whole herb is officinal.

MEDICAL PROPERTIES.

Tonic, aperient, pectoral and sudorific. Is largely employed in domestic practice in colds, asthma, catarrh, and other chronic affections of the lungs, attended with coughs and copious expectoration.

PREPARATIONS.

Fluid Extract.................................Dose, 1-2 to 1 Dram.
Solid Extract.................................. " 5 to 10 Grains
Pills...2 Grains each.

TINCTURE OF HOREHOUND.

Fluid Extract.................................Two Ounces.
Diluted Alcohol...............................One Pint.
Dose—Half to one ounce.

SYRUP OF HOREHOUND.

Fluid Extract.................................Three Ounces.
Syrup...One Pint.
Dose—Three to six drams.

MENTHA PIPERITA.

Peppermint.

A native of England, where it is largely cultivated for the sake of its oil. The whole herb is officinal.

MEDICAL PROPERTIES

It is a powerful diffusive stimulant, anti-spasmodic, carminative and stomachic. Used in flatulent colic, hysteria, spasms, or cramps in the stomach; to allay the griping of cathartics; to check nausea and vomiting, and to disguise the unpleasant taste of other medicines.

PREPARATION.

Fluid Extract.....................................Dose, 1 to 2 Drams.

INFUSION OF PEPPERMINT.

Fluid Extract.....................................One Ounce.
Water.....................................One Pint.
Dose—Four to eight ounces.

MENTHA VIRIDIS.

Spearmint.

This species is a native of Europe, but is extensively cultivated in this country for domestic use and for the sake of its oil. The whole plant is officinal.

MEDICAL PROPERTIES.

Like the last, it is carminative, anti-spasmodic, and stimulant. It is mainly used as a diuretic and febrifuge. The tincture has been found serviceable in gonorrhea, strangury, gravel, &c.

PREPARATION.

Fluid Extract.....................................Dose, 1 to 3 Drams.

TINCTURE OF SPEARMINT.

Fluid Extract.....................................Four Ounces.
Diluted Alcohol.....................................One Pint.
Dose—One-and-a-half to three drams.

INFUSION OF SPEARMINT.

Fluid Extract.....................................Two Ounces.
Water.....................................One Pint.
Dose—Two to four ounces. As a febrifuge in warm infusion, and in cold infusion beneficial in high color or scalding of urine, difficult micturition, &c.

MYRICA CERIFERA.

Bayberry.

Found in damp places in many parts of the United States; is very abundant in New Jersey. The bark of the root is officinal.

MEDICAL PROPERTIES.

Astringent and stimulant, and in large doses is apt to occasion emesis. Successfully employed in scrofula, jaundice, diarrhea, dysentery, and other diseases where an astringent stimulant is indicated. Beneficial as a gargle in sore mouth and throat.

PREPARATIONS.

Fluid Extract.................................Dose, 1 to 2 Drams.
Myricin .... " 2 to 10 Grains.

INFUSION OF BAYBERRY.

Fluid Extract.................................Two Ounces.
Water...Ten Ounces.
Dose—Three-quarters to one-and-a-half ounces.

TINCTURE OF BAYBERRY.

Fluid Extract.................................Four Ounces.
Diluted Alcohol ....Twelve Ounces.
Dose—Half to one ounce.

NEPETA CATARIA.

Catnip.

Catnip is a native of Europe, and is widely naturalized in this country. The names of this plant, in all languages, indicate the fondness of the cats for it, upon whom it is said to exert an aphrodisiac influence. The tops and leaves are officinal.

MEDICAL PROPERTIES.

Carminative and diaphoretic in warm infusion. Used in febrile diseases, in flatulent colic, nervous headache, hysteria and nervous irritability.

PREPARATION.

Fluid Extract ....Dose, 2 to 4 Drams.

INFUSION OF CATNIP.

Fluid Extract.......................................Four Ounces.
Water ....One Pint.

Dose—Two to four ounces.

MIXTURE OF CATNIP AND SAFFRON.

Fluid Extract of Catnip.........................Two Ounces.
" " " Saffron ....One-and-a-half Oz.

Dose—One-and-a-half to three drams. Popular remedy in colds, febrile and exanthematous diseases to which infants and young children are subject.

CATNIP MIXTURE.

Fluid Extract of Catnip.........................Six Drams.
" " " Valerian ....Four "
" " " Scullcap .... " "

Dose—One to three drams. Excellent in nervous headache, restlessness, and many other nervous symptoms

OPIUM.

Opium is prepared from the unripe capsules of the *Papaver Somniferum*, and presents many varieties, as the Turkey or Smyrna, the East Indian or Bengal, the Egyptian, &c.; of which, the first is the best, and affords the largest proportion of morphia.

MEDICAL PROPERTIES

The Fluid Extract of opium (Aqueous) is of the same strength as laudanum, and is largely used in its stead; is anodyne in its action, promotes sleep, allays spasms and convulsions, and is valuable in nervous irritability. It can be used where laudanum or opium is generally applicable, without the unpleasant effects that usually follow from either. The fluid opium is denarcotized; prepared according to the formula of Prof. Proctor.

PREPARATION.

Fluid Extract of Opium (Aqueous).................Dose 10 to 60 Drops.

WINE OF AQUEOUS OPIUM.

Fluid Extract.......................................Two Ounces.
Sherry Wine.......................................Fourteen Ounces.

Dose—One to four drams.

PAPAVER SOMNIFERUM.

Poppy.

Supposed to be a native of Persia. The dried capsules are the parts used in medicine.

MEDICAL PROPERTIES.

The Poppy heads, though analogous to opium in medical properties, are exceedingly feeble. They are often given internally to calm irritation, to promote rest, and produce, generally, the narcotic effects of opium.

PREPARATIONS.

Fluid Extract........................ .Dose, 1-2 to 1 Dram.
Solid Extract .... " 3 to 10 Grains.
Pills.................................... ....2 Grains each.

SYRUP OF POPPY.

Fluid Extract................................Four Ounces.
Syrup ....Twelve Ounces.
Dose—Two to four drams.

PHYTOLACCA DECANDRA.

Poke.

The Poke is abundant in all parts of the United States, as well as in the north of Africa and south of Europe. The leaves, berries and root are used in medicine, but the two latter only are mentioned in the Pharmacopeia. The root is the most active.

MEDICAL PROPERTIES.

It is a slow emetic, purgative, and somewhat narcotic. Used in chronic and syphilitic rheumatism, and for allaying syphilitic pains. It is said to be a sure cure for syphilis in all its stages, without the use of mercury. Acts as an alterative in scrofula and scrofulous diseases.

PREPARATIONS.

Fluid Extract................................Dose, 10 to 30 Drops.
Solid Extract .... " 1 to 4 Grains.
Phytolaccin...................... .... " 1-4 to 1 Grain.
Pills of Phytolacca.............................1 Grain each.
" " Phytolaccin.............................1-2 Grain each

TINCTURE OF POKE.

Fluid Extract....................................Four Ounces.
Diluted Alcohol....................................One Pint.

Dose—Half to one dram.

SYRUP OF POKE.

Fluid Extract ....Two Ounces.
Syrup ....Fourteen Ounces.

Dose—One to two drams.

COMPOUND WINE OF POKE.

Fluid Extract....................................Half Ounce.
White Turpentine....................................Half Ounce.
Sherry Wine....................................Two Pints.

Dose—Half to one dram.

OINTMENT OF POKE.

Solid Extract ....Two Ounces.
Lard....................................Half pound.

COMPOUND PILLS OF POKE.

Solid Extract of Poke....................................Two Drams.
" " " Stillingia....................................One Dram.
" " " Stramonium....................................Eight Grains.

Mix, and divide into sixty pills. Dose—One pill every two, three or four hours. Useful in osteocopus, mercurial or syphitic pain in the bones, rheumatism, syphilis, and scrofula.

PIPER ANGUSTIFOLIUM.

Matico.

This plant was discovered on the 9th of December, 1824, by the Spanish soldier whose name it bears. He was bleeding to death when he accidentally caught hold of the plant and brought some of the leaves in contact with the wound, which immediately arrested the hemorrhage.

MEDICAL PROPERTIES.

Principally styptic, also stimulant. Of advantage in epistaxis, leucorrhea, menorrhagia, chronic diarrhea, and diseases of the mucous membranes. As a local styptic it acts in the same manner as agaric.

PREPARATION.

Fluid Extract....................................Dose, 1-2 to 2 Drams.

TINCTURE OF MATICO.

Fluid Extract....................................Eight Ounces.
Diluted Alcohol....................................Two Pints.

Dose—Two to eight drams.

INFUSION OF MATICO.

Fluid Extract....................................Half Ounce.
Water ....Half Pint.

Dose—One to two ounces.

SYRUP OF MATICO.

Fluid Extract....................................Four Ounces.
Diluted Alcohol.................................... " "
Syrup....................................Eight "

Dose—Two to four drams.

INFUSION OF MATICO AND SENNA.

Fluid Extract of Matico....................................Two Drams.
" " " Senna....................................Two Drams.
Water ....One Pint.

Dose—One-and-a-half to three ounces. *Waternough.*

PIPER CUBEBA.

Cubebs.

Native of Java and other East India islands, where it grows wild in the woods. The dried unripe fruit is the officinal portion.

MEDICAL PROPERTIES.

Cubebs is gently stimulant, with particular direction to the urinary organs; has the power of arresting excessive discharges from the urethra; used principally in the treatment of gonorrhea and gleet; also used beneficially in leucorrhea, abscess of the prostate glands, piles, and chronic bronchial inflammation, &c.

PREPARATIONS.

Fluid Extract of Cubebs....................................Dose, 1-2 to 1 1-2 Drams.
" " " " Etherial.................................... " 1 to 2 Drams.
Solid Extract .... " 2 to 20 Grains.
Pills of Ext. Cubebs and Copaiba....................................3 Grains each.
" " " " " " and Citrate of Iron.3 " "
" " " " " Alum....................................3 " "
" " " " " Ext. of Rhatany and Iron.3 " "
" " Ext. Cubeba....................................2 Grains each.

TINCTURE OF CUBEBS.

Fluid Extract..................................Two Ounces.
Diluted Alcohol................................One Pint.

Dose—One to two drams.

MIXTURE OF CUBEBS AND ERGOT.

Fluid Extract of Cubebs.....................Five Drams.
" " " Ergot....................One-and-a-half Drams.
Cinnamon Water.............................Half Dram.
Powdered Sugar.............................One Dram.

Dose—One dram. In gonorrhea, gleet, leucorrhea, &c.

PIPER NIGRUM.

Black Pepper.

This plant grows wild in Cochin-China and various parts of India. The berries are officinal.

MEDICAL PROPERTIES.

The Black Pepper is a warm carminative stimulant, having the property of producing general arterial excitement. Its chief medicinal application is to excite the languid stomach and correct flatulence.

PREPARATIONS.

Fluid Extract..................................Dose, 10 to 40 Drops.
Pills of Piperin...........................Half Grain each.

TINCTURE OF BLACK PEPPER.

Fluid Extract..................................Two Ounces.
Diluted Alcohol................................One Pint.

Dose—Half to one-and-a-half drams.

SYRUP OF BLACK PEPPER.

Fluid Extract..................................Four Ounces.
Syrup..Twelve Ounces.

Dose—Quarter [illegible] dram.

COMPOUND PILLS OF PIPERIN.

Pil. Hydrarg...................................One Grain.
Piperin..Two Grains.
Sulphate of Quinia.............................Two Grains.
Syrup..Sufficient.

Dose—One to be taken morning, noon and night. *Harth.*

PODOPHYLLUM PELTATUM.

Mandrake.

The Peltatum is the only species strictly belonging to this genus. Found exclusively in America. The root is the officinal portion.

MEDICAL PROPERTIES.

It is a certain cathartic; in large doses an emetic, alterative, anthelmintic, hydragogue and sialogogue. It rouses the liver to vigorous action, determines the blood to the surface, stimulates the kidneys, promotes expectoration, augments the glandular functions, and cleanses the intestinal canal of all irritating substances. In small doses it acts as a powerful alterative. Useful in scrofulous and syphilitic diseases, hepatic affections, dysmenorrhea, rheumatism, gonorrhea; also administered beneficially in jaundice, dropsies, dysentery, diarrhea, bilious, remittent and intermittent fevers, puerperal fever, typhoid fever, and all glandular enlargements. Its range of application is perhaps more extensive than any other cathartic medicine, and is indicated in all cases where the use of mercury is indicated.

PREPARATIONS.

Fluid Extract........................Dose, 1-2 to 1 Dram.
" " Compound............. " 1 to 2 Drams.
Solid Extract...................... " 3 to 12 Grains.
Podophyllin......................... " 1-8 to 1-4 and 1 to 3 Grains.
Pills of Podophyllin...................1-2 Grain.
" " Ext. Podophyllum............1 Grain.
" " Podophyllin and Blue Mass....3 Grains.

TINCTURE OF PODOPHYLLUM.

Fluid Extract...............................Three Ounces.
Alcohol.......................................Thirteen Ounces.
Dose—One-and-a-half to four drams.

1.

COMPOUND PILLS.

Solid Extract of Podophyllum...................Half Dram.
Podophyllin ....Ten Grains.
Mix, and divide into ten pills. Dose—One, every three hours

2.

Podophyllin...................................One Dram.
Scammony.....................................One "
Gamboge ....One "

Castile Soap....................................Half Dram.

Mix well, and divide into 120 pills. Dose—One or two.

3

Solid Extract Mandrake........................One Ounce.
" " Dandelion........................ " "
" Conium.......................... " "

Mix. Divide into three-grain pills. Dose—Two to three. Valuable in hepatic and bilious difficulties.

4

Podophyllin...............................Four Grains.
Iridin.................................Four "
Strychnia ....One-and-a-half Grains.
Solid Extract of Belladonna................Five Grains.
Conserve of Roses.................... ......Sufficient.

Mix, and form twenty pills. Dose—One, three times a day, using in combination, active diuretic infusions. Useful in urethral strictures and recent diseases of the prostate glands.

Podophyllin....................................One Part.
Leptandrin....................................Ten Parts.
Sugar ....Ten Parts.

Dose—Two grains. Excellent alterative in dyspepsia.

Podophyllin....................................Four Grains.
Blue Mass.....................................Twenty Grains.

Mix, and make into eight pills.

Podophyllin....................................Half Dram.
White Turpentine..........................Half "
Carbonate of Iron...............................One "

Mix well, and divide into thirty pills. *Eclec. Med. Journal.*

Podophyllin....................................One Dram.
Scammony, in Powder..........................One "
Gamboge, " " ....One "

Rub together for half an hour, and add

Castile Soap....................................Half Dram.

Beat into a mass, and make 120 pills. *Eclec. Med. Journal.*

MANDRAKE COMPOUND.

Compounded of Mandrake, Senna and Jalap.

POLYGONUM PUNCTATUM.

Water Pepper.

The Polygonum is found growing in nearly all parts of the United States, in low grounds, ditches, among rubbish, and about brooks and water courses. The whole plant is officinal, and has a pungent, biting, acrid taste.

MEDICAL PROPERTIES.

Stimulant, diuretic, emmenagogue, antiseptic, and vesicant. Used in colds, coughs, gravel, uterine diseases, &c.

PREPARATIONS.

Fluid Extract.................................Dose, 10 to 60 Drops.
Solid Extract.................................. " 2 to 3 Grains.

TINCTURE OF WATER PEPPER.

Fluid Extract ....Four Ounces.
Diluted Alcohol ....One Pint.
Dose—Half to two drams, three or four times a day.

INFUSION OF WATER PEPPER.

Fluid Extract..............................Half Ounce.
Water ....One Pint.
Dose—Half to one ounce.

COMPOUND PILLS OF WATER PEPPER.

Dried Sulphate of Iron........................One Dram.
Cimicifugin....................................One Dram.
Iridin ....Fifteen Grains.
Solid Extract of Water Pepper..................Sufficient.

Mix, and divide into sixty pills. Dose—One pill every two or three hours. These pills are emmenagogue, and exert an especial influence on the female organs of generation.

POLYGALA SENEGA,

Seneka.

The root of this indigenous plant is the part used in medicine. Usually called Seneca Snakeroot.

MEDICAL PROPERTIES.

Seneka is a stimulating diuretic and expectorant, and in large doses emetic and cathartic. It excites more or less all the secretions. It is peculiarly useful in chronic catarrhal affections, the secondary stages of croup, and in peripneumonia.

PREPARATION.

Fluid Extract.................................Dose, 20 to 40 Drops.

INFUSION OF SENEKA.

Fluid Extract of Seneka........................One Ounce.
Water.......................................One Pint.
Dose—One to one-and-a-half ounces.

SYRUP OF SENEKA

Fluid Extract..................................Four Ounces.
Syrup.......................................Twelve Ounces.
Dose—Half to one dram.

SYRUP OF SENEKA, SQUILL, AND IPECAC.

Fluid Extract of Seneka........................Two Drams.
" " " Squill..........................Two "
" " " Ipecac.........................Four "
Syrup.......................................Three Ounces.
Dose—One dram every three hours. This combines the expectorant properties of the seneka and squill, with the relaxing effect of the ipecac.

SYRUP OF TOLU, WITH SENEKA, BELLADONNA, &c.

Fluid Extract of Seneka...................One Dram.
" " " Belladonna..............Half Dram.
" " " Ipecac...................Thirty Drops.
Syrup of Tolu........................Three-and-a-half Ounces.
Syrup..............................Seven Drams.
Sherry Wine.........................One Dram.
Dose—One dram three times a day, freely using gum water acidulated with lemon juice. In coughs.

1.
EXPECTORANT COMPOUNDS OF SENEKA.

Fluid Extract of Seneka...................Two Drams.
Iodide of Potash.........................Two "
Antimonial Wine ....Four "

Syrup of Tolu .... One-and-a-half Ounces.
Water .... Three-and-a-half Ounces.

Dose—One dram.

2.

Fluid Extract of Seneka .... Two Drams.
" " " Ipecac .... One Dram.
Honey .... Two Ounces.
Water .... Six Ounces.

Dose—One dram.

3

Fluid Extract of Seneka .... Three Drams.
" " " Squill .... Half Dram.
Syrup of Tolu .... Two Drams.
Paregoric .... Two Drams.
Carbonate of Ammonia .... Twenty Grains.
Water .... Four-and-a-half Oz.

Dose—One dram.

POPULUS TREMULOIDES.

American Poplar.

This tree is common in Lower Canada, and in the Northern and Middle States. The bark is officinal.

MEDICAL PROPERTIES.

Tonic and febrifuge ; has been used in intermittent fever with advantage. An infusion is reputed a valuable remedy in debility, want of appetite, feeble digestion, chronic diarrhea and worms. It is said to possess active diuretic properties.

PREPARATION.

Populin .... Dose, 4 to 8 Grains.

PRINOS VERTICILLATUS.

Black Alder.

This species of Prinos grows in all parts of the United States, from Canada to Florida. The bark is officinal, though sometimes the berries are used medicinally for the same purposes.

MEDICAL PROPERTIES

The Black Alder has been used with good effect in jaundice, diarrhea, intermittent fever, and other diseases connected with a debilitated state of the system, especially gangrene and mortification. It is a popular remedy in gangrenous or flabby and ill-conditioned ulcers, and in chronic cutaneous eruptions, in which it is given internally, and applied locally in the form of a wash or poultice.

PREPARATION.

Fluid Extract.................................... Dose, 1 to 2 Drams

TINCTURE OF BLACK ALDER.

Fluid Extract.................................Two Ounces.
Diluted Alcohol...............................One Pint.
Dose—Two to four drams.

SYRUP OF BLACK ALDER.

Fluid Extract.................................Four Ounces.
Syrup...Twelve Ounces.
Dose—One to two drams.

LOTION OF BLACK ALDER.

Fluid Extract.................................Three Ounces.
Water...Eight Ounces.

COMPOUND INFUSION OF BLACK ALDER.

Fluid Extract of Black Alder.....................Two Drams.
" " " Golden Seal.................One Dram.
Water...One Pint.
Dose—Four fluid ounces. Valuable in dyspepsia.

PRUNUS VIRGINIANA.

Wild Cherry.

This is one of the largest productions of the American forest, flourishing most where the soil is fertile and the climate temperate. The inner bark is the part employed in medicine.

MEDICAL PROPERTIES.

Tonic and stimulant in operation on the digestive organs, at the same time exercising a sedative influence on the circulatory and nervous systems.

It is useful in the convalescent stages of inflammatory attacks, and in many pulmonary diseases, imparting tonicity without exciting, unduly, the heart and blood vessels. It is of general use in phthisis, scrofula and dyspepsia.

PREPARATIONS.

Fluid Extract of Wild Cherry........................Dose, 2 to 4 Drams.
" " Compound.............. " 1-2 to 2 Drams.
Prunin..2 to 6 Grains.
Wine of Wild Cherry.

INFUSION OF WILD CHERRY.

Fluid Extract..................................Half Ounce.
Water..One Pint.
Dose—Two ounces, two to four times a day.

SYRUP OF WILD CHERRY.

Fluid Extract..................................Three Ounces.
Syrup..Thirteen Ounces.
Dose—Two drams to one ounce.

CHERRY COMPOUND.

Compounded of Cherry, Hoarhound, Lettuce, Veratrum, Bloodroot.

PYROLA ROTUNDIFOLIA.

Wintergreen.

Common in damp and shady woods, throughout various parts of the United States. The whole plant is used in medicine.

MEDICAL PROPERTIES.

Tonic, astringent, diuretic, and anti-spasmodic. Used in a carcinomatous or scrofulous taint of the system, in leucorrhea, and, both internally and externally, in various cutaneous eruptions. Said to be valuable in many urinary affections, as gravel, hematuria, and ulceration of the bladder.

PREPARATION.

Fluid Extract....................................Dose, 1 to 2 Drams.

INFUSION OF WINTERGREEN.

Fluid Extract ....Two Ounces.
Water..One Pint.
Dose—Two or three ounces. Also used as wash.

QUERCUS ALBA.

White Oak.

The White Oak is a forest tree attaining the height of from sixty to ninety feet, growing throughout the Union, but is more abundant in the middle States. The bark is officinal.

MEDICAL PROPERTIES.

Tonic, astringent and alterative. As an astringent it is very valuable; given in intermittent fevers, obstinate and chronic diarrhea, used as a gargle, and in baths for children. Applied externally as an ointment to ill-conditioned ulcers, piles, &c.

PREPARATIONS.

Fluid Extract.................................Dose, 1-2 to 1 Dram.
Solid Extract................................. " 10 to 20 Grains.
Pills..2 Grains each.

TINCTURE OF WHITE OAK.

Fluid Extract..................................Two Ounces.
Diluted Alcohol................................One Pint.

Dose—Half to one ounce.

COMPOUND INFUSION OF WHITE OAK.

Fluid Extract of White Oak.....................One Ounce.
" " " Blue Flag......................Two Drams.
" " " Gentian........................Two Drams.
Water..Seven Ounces.

Dose—Six drams.

SYRUP OF WHITE OAK.

Fluid Extract..................................Two Ounces.
Syrup..Fourteen Ounces.

Dose—Four drams to one ounce.

GARGLE OF WHITE OAK.

Fluid Extract..................................One-and-a-half Ounces.
Alum...Half Dram.
Brandy...One Pint.

Ellis.

RHAMNUS CATHARTICUS.

Buckthorn.

This plant is a native of Europe, and is occasionally met with in this country. European practitioners hold it in high esteem. The berries and juice are possessed of active properties.

MEDICAL PROPERTIES.

A powerful hydragogue and purgative. Seldom used alone.

PREPARATION.

Fluid Extract.................................. Dose, 1 to 1 1-2 Dram.

SYRUP OF BUCKTHORN.

Fluid Extract.................................Four Ounces.
Syrup...Twelve Ounces.
Dose—Two ounces.

RHEUM PALMATUM.

Rhubarb.

The species from which this medicinal drug is obtained inhabit the great plains of Tartary, the Steppes of Siberia and the great ranges of mountains lying between these and the northern part of India The root is the part used in medicine.

MEDICAL PROPERTIES.

Used as a purgative in mild cases of diarrhea, and cholera infantum ; as a stomachic and tonic in dyspepsia, accompanied with debilitated condition of the digestive organs ; as a purgative for infants it is valuable and is well adapted to a variety of children's complaints.

PREPARATIONS.

Fluid Ext. of Rhubarb.........................	Dose,	1-2 to 1 Dram.
" " " " Aromatic	"	1-2 to 1 "
" " " " and Senna	"	1-2 to 1 "
Solid Extract	"	2 to 10 Grains.

Pills of Ext. Rhubarb	1 Grain each.
" " " " and Magnesia	2 Grains "
" " " " and Iron	3 " "
" " Rhubarb Compound (U. S. P.)	4 " "
" " Ext. Rhubarb and Blue Mass	3 " "

TINCTURE OF RHUBARB.

Fluid Extract	Three Ounces.
Essence of Cardamom	Half Ounce.
Diluted Alcohol	Two Pints.

Dose—Half to one-and-a-half ounces.

INFUSION OF RHUBARB.

Fluid Extract	One Ounce.
Spirit of Cinnamon	Two Ounces.
Water	Eighteen Ounces.

Dose—One to three ounces.

SYRUP OF RHUBARB.

Fluid Extract	Three Ounces.
Syrup	Fourteen Ounces.

Dose—Two-and-a-half to five drams.

TINCTURE OF RHUBARB AND GENTIAN.

Fluid Extract of Rhubarb	Four Ounces.
" " " Gentian	Two Ounces.
Diluted Alcohol	One Pint.

Dose—Two to four drams.

WINE OF RHUBARB.

Fluid Extract of Rhubarb	Two Ounces.
" " " Canella	One Dram.
Diluted Alcohol	Two Ounces.
Sherry Wine	One Pint.

Dose—Two-and-a-half to four drams.

PILLS OF BLUE PILL, SODA, &c.

Blue Pill	Nine Grains.
Solid Extract of Rhubarb	Two-and-a-half Grains.
Bicarbonate of Soda	Twelve Grains.
Aromatic Syrup of Rhubarb	Sufficient.

Divide into twelve pills. Dose—One, two or three times a day, as an alterative, in derangement of the liver. *Dr. Hartshorne.*

PILLS OF RHUBARB AND SULPHATE OF IRON.

Solid Extract of Rhubarb ....One-and-a-half Drams.
Sulphate of Iron..............................Half Dram.
Soap...Two Scruples.
Distilled Water..............................Sufficient.

Mix, and divide into forty pills. Dose—Three or four at bed time.

RHUBARB PILLS.

Solid Extract of Rhubarb........................One Scruple.
Blue Mass......................................One Scruple.
Pulverized Ipecac...........................Eight Grains.

Mix, and divide into ten pills. Dose—One to two pills. A mild purgative.

RHUS GLABRUM.

Sumach.

Found extensively in the United States, growing in old neglected fields, along fences, and on the borders of woods. The bark and berries are officinal.

MEDICAL PROPERTIES.

Tonic, astringent, antiseptic and diuretic. Valuable in gonorrhea, leucorrhea, diarrhea, dysentery, hectic fever, and scrofula.

PREPARATIONS.

Fluid Extract ....Dose, 1 to 2 Drams.
Rhusin.. " 1 to 2 Grains.

TINCTURE OF SUMACH.

Fluid Extract ....Four Ounces.
Diluted Alcohol............................Thirteen Ounces.

Dose—Half to one ounce.

GARGLE OF SUMACH.

Fluid Extract...............................Two Ounces.
Water..Eight Ounces.

Useful in quinsy and ulceration of the mouth and throat; also as a wash for ringworms, tetters, offensive ulcers, &c.

RUBUS VILLOSUS.

Blackberry.

Of this extensive genus, not less than twenty species are indigenous to the United States. The roots only are officinal.

MEDICAL PROPERTIES.

Tonic and strongly astringent. An excellent remedy in diarrhea, dysentery, cholera-infantum, relaxed conditions of the intestines of children, passive hemorrhage from the stomach, bowels and uterus, and in colliquative diarrhea.

PREPARATIONS.

Fluid Extract. ....Dose, 1-2 to 1 Dram.
Solid Extract.. " 4 to 6 Grains.
Pills..2 Grains each.

TINCTURE OF BLACKBERRY.

Fluid Extract..Two Ounces.
Diluted Alcohol..One Pint.

Dose—Two to four drams.

INFUSION OF BLACKBERRY.

Fluid Extract ....One Ounce.
Water..One Pint.

Dose—One ounce

SYRUP OF BLACKBERRY.

Fluid Extract..Four Ounces.
Syrup..Twelve Ounces.

Dose—Half to one ounce.

WINE OF BLACKBERRY.

Fluid Extract..Two Ounces.
Wine..Eight Ounces.

Dose—Half to one-and-a-half drams.

RUMEX CRISPUS.

Yellow Dock.

This plant is a native of Europe, introduced into this country, where it grows wild in pastures, dry fields, waste grounds, &c. The root is officinal.

MEDICAL PROPERTIES.

Alterative, tonic, mildly astringent and detergent. Useful in scorbutic and syphilitic affections, leprosy, elephantiasis, &c.

PREPARATIONS.

Fluid Extract................................Dose, 1 to 2 Drams.
Rumin................................" 4 to 8 Grains.
Solid Extract................................" 4 to 8 Grains.
Pills of Solid Extract................................2 Grains each.

SYRUP OF YELLOW DOCK.

Fluid Extract................................Four Ounces.
Syrup................................Twelve Ounces.
Dose—Half to one ounce.

RUTA GRAVEOLENS.

Rue.

This plant is a native of the south of Europe, but is cultivated in our gardens. The whole herb is active, but the leaves are usually employed.

MEDICAL PROPERTIES.

Its action is chiefly directed to the uterus; in moderate doses proving emmenagogue, and in large doses producing a degree of irritation in that organ which sometimes determines abortion. It has been successfully used in flatulent colic, hysteria, epilepsy, and is an efficient vermifuge.

PREPARATIONS.

Fluid Extract................................Dose, 20 to 40 Drops.
Solid Extract................................" 2 to 4 Grains.
Pills................................2 Grains each.

TINCTURE OF RUE.

Fluid Extract................................Four Ounces.
Diluted Alcohol................................Four Ounces.
Dose—Thirty to sixty drops. *Beral.*

SYRUP OF RUE.

Tincture of Rue....................................Two Ounces.
Distilled Water....................................Seven "
Syrup....................................Seven "
Dose—Half to one dram. *Beral.*

MIXTURE OF RUE AND SQUILL.

Fluid Extract of Rue....................................One Ounce.
Oxymel of Squill....................................Half Ounce.
Dose—Twenty-five to forty drops. In hysteric affections *Pierquin.*

SALIX ALBA.

Willow.

The White Willow has been introduced into this country from Europe, and is now very common. There are not less than a hundred and thirty species of this genus. The bark is officinal.

MEDICAL PROPERTIES.

Tonic and astringent, and has been employed as a substitute for cinchona, in intermittent fever. Useful in chronic diarrhea and dysentery. The *Salicin* is tonic, anti-spasmodic and febrifuge. It is less likely to offend the stomach and affect the nervous system than quinia.

PREPARATION.

Salicin....................................Dose, 2 to 10 Grains.

SANGUINARIA CANADENSIS.

Bloodroot.

The Bloodroot grows abundantly throughout the whole United States, flowering early in the spring. All parts of the plant are active, but the root only is officinal.

MEDICAL PROPERTIES.

Valuable as an emetic, narcotic, and stimulant. In small doses it stimulates the digestive organs, and accelerates the circulation, while in large doses it produces nausea and consequent depression of the pulse. Used in typhoid pneumonia, catarrh, pertussis, scarlatina, rheumatism, jaundice, dyspepsia, &c. Considered a specific in the early stages of croup. The Sanguinarina possesses the same properties. The Sanguinarin acts as a tonic, hepatic and alterative. May be employed to advantage in pulmonary diseases, hooping cough; as a sternutatory, and as a local application to indolent ulcers.

PREPARATIONS.

Fluid Extract..................Dose, 5 to 15 and 40 to 60 Drops.
Solid Extract.................. " 1-2 to 1 1-2 and 2 1-2 to 5 Grains.
Sanguinarina.................. " 1-30 to 1-10 Grains.
Sanguinarin.................. " 1-4 to 1 and 1-2 to 2 Grains.
Pills of Sanguinaria............1-2 Grain and 1 Grain each.
" " Sanguinarin............1-2 Grain and 1 Grain each.

TINCTURE OF BLOODROOT.

Fluid Extract................................Four Ounces.
Diluted Alcohol..............................Two Pints.

Dose—Half to one dram; as an emetic, four to eight drams.

INFUSION OF BLOODROOT.

Fluid Extract................................Half Ounce.
Water.......................................One Pint.

Dose—Two to four drams.

SYRUP OF BLOODROOT.

Fluid Extract..........................Eight Ounces.
Acetic Acid............................Four Ounces.
Syrup..................................Two-and-a-quarter Pints.

Dose—One to two drams.

COMPOUND TINCTURE OF BLOODROOT.

Fluid Extract of Bloodroot......................Two Ounces.
" " " Black Cohosh..................Four Ounces.
" " " Poke.........................One Ounce.

Dose—Half to one dram.

VINEGAR OF BLOODROOT.

Fluid Extract................................Four Ounces.
Distilled Vinegar............................Two Pints.
Alcohol......................................One Ounce.

Dose—Twenty to forty drops.

SYRUP OF BLOODROOT COMPOUND FOR COUGHS.

Fluid Extract of Bloodroot.......................Two Ounces.
" " " Squill.........................Two "
" " " Ipecac........................Two "
Balsam of Tolu...................................One-and-a-half Oz.
Paregoric..Three Ounces.
Syrup..Three Pints.

Dose—One dram wheu the cough is troublesome.

MIXTURE OF BLOODROOT AND HYDROCYANIC ACID.

Fluid Extract of Bloodroot................One Dram.
" " " Ipecac...................One Dram.
" " " Wild Cherry.............One-and-a-half Ounces.
Hydrocyanic Acid (Medicinal).... ....Sixty Drops.
Sulphate of Morphia........... ....Three Grains.
Diluted Alcohol................. ......Threc Drams.
Sherry Wine..........................Three Drams.
Syrup.................................Three-and-a-half Ounces.

Dose—One dram, two or three times a day. Valuable in chronic diseases, in allaying the cough in tuberculosis, and in all pulmonary catarrhal diseases unattended with pain. *H. Green.*

Sanguinarin.....................................Twelve Grains.
Caulophyllin .... " "
Solid Extract of Cimicifuga.................... " "

Make into four-grain pills. Efficacious in amenorrhea, dysmenorrhea, and other functional disorders of the female generative system.

SCILLA MARITIMA.

Squill.

The Squill grows in the countries bordering on the Mediterranean. The bulb is the officinal portion.

MEDICAL PROPERTIES.

Squill is expectorant, diuretic, and in large doses, emetic and purgative. As an expectorant, it is used both in cases of deficient and superabundant secretion from the bronchial mucous membrane. It is used in dropsy to increase the secretery action of the kidneys.

PREPARATIONS.

Fluid Extract of Squill......Dose, Expectorant and Diuretic, 2 to 6 Drops.
" " " " " Emetic..............12 to 24 Drops.
" " " " Compound......................10 to 20 Drops.
Pills of Squill Compound (U. S. P.)....................3 Grains each.

TINCTURE OF SQUILL.

Fluid Extract..............................Two Ounces.
Diluted Alcohol..............................One Pint.
Dose—Twenty to forty drops.

SYRUP OF SQUILL.

Fluid Extract..............................One Ounce.
Syrup..............................One Pint.
Dose—Quarter to half a dram.

MIXTURE OF SQUILL AND IPECAC

Fluid Extract of Squill........................One Dram.
" " " Ipecac........................Two Drams.
Dose—Ten to thirty drops.

MIXTURE OF SQUILL AND CONIUM.

Fluid Extract of Squill........................One Dram.
" " " Conium........................One Dram.
Water of Ammonia........................Three Drams.
Dose—Ten to forty drops.

MIXTURE OF SQUILL AND HYOSCYAMUS.

Fluid Extract of Squill....................Half Dram.
" " " Hyoscyamus..............Two-thirds Dram.
Tincture of Myrrh........................One-and-a-half Drams.
Water..............................One Ounce.
Dose—Half to one-and-a-half drams.

WINE OF SQUILL.

Fluid Extract..............................One Ounce.
White Wine..............................One Pint.
Dose—Half to one ounce.

VINEGAR OF SQUILL

Fluid Extract..............................Two Ounces.
Diluted Acetic Acid..............................One Pint.
Dose—Twenty to forty drops.

COMPOUND SYRUP OF SQUILL.

Hive Syrup.

Fluid Ext. Squill Compound .... Eight Ounces.
Tart. Ant. and Potassa........................ Forty-Eight Grains.
Syrup.................................. Two-and-a-half Pints.

Dose—Ten drops to one dram, according to age.

SQUILL COMPOUND.

Compounded of Squill and Seneka.

SCUTELLARIA LATERIFLORA.

Scullcap.

Scullcap is an indigenous herb, flowering in July and August. The whole plant is officinal.

MEDICAL PROPERTIES.

Scullcap is a valuable nervine. Those who have long used it, claim for it tonic properties, which give strength as well as quiet to the system, and that it does not, like other nervines, leave the system in an excited and irritable condition. It has also sudorific and diuretic properties. Used in tic-doloureux, St. Vitus dance, convulsions, tetanus, as well as in ordinary diseases of the nerves.

PREPARATIONS.

Fluid Extract.................................. Dose, 1-2 to 1 Dram.
" " of Scullcap Compound.............. " 1-2 to 1 Dram.
Scutellarin.................................. " 2 to 6 Grains.
Pills of Scutellarin.... .... 1 Grain each.

INFUSION OF SCULLCAP.

Fluid Extract.................................. One Ounce.
Water.. One Pint.

In doses of a wine-glassful three times a day, it has entirely cured tic-doloureux.

SCULLCAP COMPOUND.

Compounded of Scullcap, Ladies's Slipper, Hop, Lettuce.

SENECIO AUREUS.

Life Root.

This is an indigenous perennial plant, growing on the banks of creeks and in low marshy grounds, throughout the northern and western parts of the Union, flowering in May and June. The root and herb are the officinal parts.

MEDICAL PROPERTIES.

Diuretic, pectoral, diaphoretic and tonic. An excellent remedy in gravel and other urinary affections; is said to be a specific in strangury; very efficacious in promoting menstrual discharges, and a valuable agent in the treatment of female diseases. The *Senecin* possesses, to a high degree, the virtues of the plant whence it is derived.

PREPARATIONS.

Fluid Extract.................................Dose, 1-2 to 1 Dram
Senecin..." 3 to 5 Grains.

INFUSION OF LIFE ROOT

Fluid Extract.................................One Ounce.
Water..One Pint.

Dose—One to four ounces.

Senecin...Four Grains.
Aletrin..." "
Sulphate of Iron.............................." "

Make into two-grain powders. In chlorosis accompanied by amenorrhea.

Senecin...Ten Grains.
Sulphate of Quinia..........................Six Grains.
Solid Extract of Belladonna...............Three Grains.
Conserve of Roses...........................Sufficient.

Make into ten pills. In dysmenorrhea.

Senecin...Six Grains.
Geraniin.." "

Dose—Two to four grains. In menorrhagia.

SIMARUBA EXCELSA.

Quassia.

This species inhabits Jamaica and the Carribbean Islands, where it is called *bitter ash*. The wood is the part used in medicine.

MEDICAL PROPERTIES.

It possesses in the highest degree all the properties of simple bitters. It is purely tonic, invigorating the digestive organs, with little excitement of the circulation, or increase of animal heat. Particularly adapted to dyspepsia and to that debilitated state of the digestive organs which sometimes succeeds acute disease.

PREPARATIONS.

Fluid Extract.................................Dose, 1-2 to 1 Dram.
Solid Extract.................................. " 3 to 5 Grains.
Pills...1 Grain each.

TINCTURE OF QUASSIA.

Fluid Extract.................................Two Ounces.
Diluted Alcohol...............................Two Pints.
Dose—Four to eight drams.

INFUSION OF QUASSIA.

Fluid Extract.................................Two Drams.
Water...One Pint.
Dose—Four to six drams.

COMPOUND INFUSION OF QUASSIA.

Fluid Extract of Quassia......................Half Ounce.
" " " Snakeroot...............................Half "
" " " Orange Peel.............................Half "
Water...Two Pints.
Dose—Half to one-and-a-half ounces.

WINE OF QUASSIA.

Fluid Extract of Quassia......................Half Ounce.
" " " Orange Peel.............................Two Drams.
Sherry Wine...................................One-and-a-half Pints.
Dose—Two to four ounces.

SMILAX OFFICINALIS.

Sarsaparilla.

This species is indigenous, growing in swamps and hedges in the Middle and Southern States. The root is the part used in medicine.

MEDICAL PROPERTIES

Possesses a high reputation as an alterative in the treatment of chronic rheumatism, scrofulous affections, cutaneous affections, syphiloid diseases, and that depraved condition of the general health to which it is difficult to apply a name.

PREPARATIONS.

Fluid Extract of Sarsaparilla,	Rio Negro...........	Dose,	1 Dram.
" " " "	Compound (U. S. P.)..	"	1 "
" " " "	and Dandelion.......	"	1 "
Solid Extract " "	Amer..	"	5 to 20 Grains.
" " " "	" Compound.....	"	5 to 20 "
" " " "	Rio Negro...........	"	5 to 15 "
" " " "	" Compound...	"	5 to 15 "

Pills of each of the Solid Extracts...............3 Grains each.

INFUSION OF SARSAPARILLA.

Fluid Extract.................................One Ounce.
Water ....One Pint.

Dose—Two to four ounces.

SYRUP OF SARSAPARILLA.

Fluid Extract.................................Two Ounces.
Syrup...Fourteen Ounces.

Dose—One to two ounces.

Syrup of the Sarsaparilla Compound made similarly, and administered in like doses.

SARSAPARILLA COMPOUND.

Compounded of Sarsaparilla, Prince's Pine, Liquorice, Mezereon, Sassafras, Yellow Dock, and Bittersweet.

SOLANUM DULCAMARA.

Bittersweet.

Common in Europe and North America. The root and stalk have medicinal properties, though the latter only is officinal.

MEDICAL PROPERTIES.

Chiefly used in syrup or infusion in cutaneous diseases, scrofula, jaundice, syphilitic, rheumatic and cachectic affections, leucorrhea and obstructed menstruation. Possesses feeble narcotic powers and increases the secretions of the kidneys and the skin. It is especially beneficial in the treatment of cutaneous eruptions of a scaly character. Antaphrodisiac properties are ascribed to it, rendering it useful in mania connected with strong venereal propensities.

PREPARATIONS.

Fluid Extract. ....Dose, 1-2 to 1 Dram.
Solid Extract................................. " 3 to 8 Grains.
Pills ....2 Grains each.

INFUSION OF BITTERSWEET.

Fluid Extract.................................One Ounce.
Water ....One Pint.
Dose—One to two ounces, three or four times a day

COMPOUND INFUSION OF BITTERSWEET.

Fluid Extract of Bittersweet...................One Ounce.
" " " Burdock.......................Half "
" " " Sassafras..................... " "
" " Yellow Dock.................... " "
Water..One Pint.
Dose—One to two ounces.

COMPOUND SYRUP OF BITTERSWEET.

Same as above, substituting syrup for the water.

SYRUP OF BITTERSWEET.

Fluid Extract ....Four Ounces.
Syrup..Twelve Ounces.
Dose—Four drams.

MIXTURE OF BITTERSWEET.

Fluid Extract of Bittersweet................Two Ounces.
" " " Yellow Dock............... " "
" " " Stillingia.................. " "
Syrup..................................One-and-a-half Pints.

Dose—One to two drams, in scrofulous and syphilitic affections.

SPIGELIA MARILANDICA.

Pink Root.

Native of the southern and southwestern States. The root alone is recognized by the Pharmacopeias.

MEDICAL PROPERTIES.

Powerful anthelmintic. In large doses acts as a cathartic, though unequal and uncertain in its operation. Over doses excite the circulation and determine to the brain, giving rise to vertigo, dimness of vision, &c. Should be given with other cathartics, as the narcotic effects are less when the medicine purges.

PREPARATIONS.

Fluid Extract of Pink Root....................Dose, 1-2 to 1 1-2 Drams.
" " " " " Compound......... " 1-2 to 2 Drams.
" " " " " and Senna......... " 1-2 to 1 Dram.

INFUSION OF PINK ROOT.

Fluid Extract..................................Half Ounce.
Water...One Pint.

Dose—Two to six ounces.

PINK ROOT COMPOUND.

Compounded of Pink Root, Senna, Savin, and Manna.

SPIRÆA TOMENTOSA.

Hardhack.

A beautiful shrub, with spikes of rose-colored flowers, and leaves of a dark-green color above and white beneath. Common in the United States.

MEDICAL PROPERTIES.

Tonic astringent. In consequence of its tonic power, it is peculiarly adapted in cases of debility; and from the same cause, should not be given during the existence of inflammatory action or febrile excitement. As an astringent it is administered in diarrhea, cholera-infantum, and other complaints where astringents are usually indicated, and is said to be less liable to disagree with the stomach than other astringents. Is an excellent remedy for summer complaints of children.

PREPARATIONS.

Fluid Extract ....Dose, 4 to 20 Drops.
Pills..2 Grains each.

STILLINGIA SYLVATICA.

Queen's Root.

The plant is found growing in pine-barrens and sandy soils from Virginia to Florida; in Mississippi and Louisiana, flowering from April to July. The root is the officinal portion.

MEDICAL PROPERTIES.

Stillingia has reputation as an alterative, and as such is used in syphilitic affections, ordinarily requiring the use of mercury; is emetic and cathartic in large doses. It has been used with efficacy in secondary syphillis, scrofula, cutaneous diseases, chronic hepatic affections, and other complaints generally benefited by alteratives. Its success leaves no doubt that it is possessed of very valuable properties.

PREPARATIONS.

Fluid Extract of Stillingia...................... Dose, 5 to 15 Drops.
" " " " Compound .... " 1-2 to 1 Dram.
Stillingin.................................... " 2 to 5 Grains.
Pills of Stillingin.............................1 Grain each.

TINCTURE OF STILLINGIA.

Fluid Extract..............................Two Ounces
Diluted Alcohol............................One Pint.
Dose—1-3 to 1 1-2 drams.

INFUSION OF STILLINGIA.

Fluid Extract..............................One Ounce.
Water ....One Pint.
Dose—One to two drams.

SYRUP OF STILLINGIA.

Fluid Extract of Stillingia.. ....Three Ounces.
" " " Prickly Ash................One-and-a-half Ounces.
Syrup..................................Six-and-a-half Ounces.

Dose—Half to one-and-a-half drams.

COMPOUND SYRUP OF STILLINGIA.

Fluid Extract of Stillingia..................Two Ounces.
" " " Bloodroot..................Two "
" " " Cherry Bark................Two "
Balsam of Tolu............................One-and-a-half Ounces.
Syrup...................................Two-and-a-half Pints.

Dose—One to two drams in chronic, bronchial and catarrhal affections.

STILLINGIA COMPOUND.

Compounded of Stillingia, Turkey Corn, Blue Flag, Prince's Pine, Prickly Ash, Yellow Dock.

STRYCHNOS IGNATIA.

St. Ignatius' Bean.

This is a native of Cochin-China, the Phillipine Islands, and other parts of Asia.

MEDICAL PROPERTIES.

It is applicable in the wide range of symptoms known as dyspeptic. It has a tonic, stimulating effect on all the organs connected with the digestive functions, by its acting directly on their nervous energies, exciting and equalizing their weakened and disturbed action. It possesses a large amount of strychnia, the active principle of the Nux Vomica.

PREPARATIONS.

Fluid Extract..............................Dose, 5 to 10 Drops.
Solid Extract.............................. " 1-2 to 1 1-2 Grains.
Pills.......................................1-2 Grain each.

WINE OF IGNATIA.

Fluid Extract..................................One Ounce.
Sherry Wine...................................One Pint.

Dose—One to two drams.

COMPOUND WINE.

Fluid Extract of Ignatia........................Three Drams.
" " " Cannabis....................Three Drams.
Sherry Wine....................................One Pint.
Dose—Half to two drams.

COMPOUND PILLS OF IGNATIA.

Solid Extract of Ignatia........................Half Scruple.
" " " Savin..........................Half Scruple.
" " " Gentian........................One Dram.
Iodide of Iron..................................One Dram.
Make into forty pills. Dose—Two pills, three times a day in chlorosis. Accompany the medicine by frequent friction of the spine and extremities, with the tincture of camphor. *T. C. Miller, M.D.*

STRYCHNOS NUX VOMICA.

Nux Vomica.

This species of the Strychnos is a moderate sized tree, a native of many parts of the East Indies, abounding particularly on the Malabar and Coromandel coasts. It owes its active medicinal properties to the presence of strychnia and brucia. The seeds are officinal.

MEDICAL PROPERTIES.

Nux Vomica is a violent excitant of the cerebro-spinal system, and, in large doses, is an active poison. In small doses, frequently repeated, it is tonic, diuretic, and even laxative. It is employed principally in the treatment of paralysis. It is said to be more beneficial in general palsy and paraplegia, than in hemiplegia, and has also been found of benefit in local palsies, as of the bladder, likewise in amaurosis, spermatorrhea, and impotence.

PREPARATIONS.

Fluid Extract....................................Dose, 5 to 15 Drops.
Solid Extract.................................... " 1-2 to 1 grain.

TINCTURE OF NUX VOMICA.

Fluid Extract...................................Four Ounces.
Alcohol...One Pint.
Dose—

FERRUGINOUS PILLS OF NUX VOMICA.

Solid Extract of Nux Vomica.....................Six Grains.
Black Oxide of Iron.............................One Dram.
Make twenty-four pills.

PILLS OF NUX VOMICA AND QUINIA.

Solid Extract of Nux Vomica..................Six Grains.
Sulphate of Quinia..........................Twenty-four Grains.
Ext. Hyoscyamus............................Twelve Grains.

Mix, and divide into twenty-four pills.

PILLS OF NUX VOMICA AND ALOES.

Solid Ext. Nux Vomica......................Half Grain.
Aloes.....................................Three-quarters Grain.
Solid Ext. Rhubarb......................... " " "

Make two pills.

SYMPLOCARPUS FŒTIDUS.

Skunk Cabbage.

This is an indigenous plant, growing abundantly in various parts of the United States. The root is officinal.

MEDICAL PROPERTIES.

Stimulant, antispasmodic, expectorant, and slightly narcotic. In large doses it will occasion nausea, vomiting, vertigo, and dimness of sight. Useful in asthma, hooping cough, nervous irritability, hysteria, epilepsy, chronic catarrh, pulmonary and bronchial affections.

PREPARATION.

Fluid Extract.................................Dose, 20 to 80 Drops.

TINCTURE OF SKUNK CABBAGE.

Fluid Extract..............................Three Ounces.
Diluted Alcohol............................One Pint.

Dose—Half to one dram

INFUSION OF SKUNK CABBAGE.

Fluid Extract..............................One Ounce.
Water......................................One Pint.

Dose—One to two ounces.

SYRUP OF SKUNK CABBAGE.

Fluid Extract..............................Two Ounces.
Syrup......................................Eight Ounces.

Dose—Two to three drams.

COMPOUND TINCTURE OF SKUNK CABBAGE.

Fluid Extract of Skunk Cabbage................One Ounce.
" " " Lobelia...................... " "
" " " Bloodroot.................... " "
" " " Pleurisy Root................ " "
" " " Ginger....................... " "
Water......................................One Pint.
Alcohol....................................Three Pints.

Dose—Two to four drams, in croup, cough, asthma, &c., to promote expectoration and remove tightness across the chest.

TARAXACUM DENS-LEONIS.

Dandelion.

This species grows spontaneously in most parts of the globe. The Pharmacopeias recognize the root only as medicinal, this being by far the most efficacious part.

MEDICAL PROPERTIES.

Valuable alterative, tonic, diuretic, and aperient. It has a specific action on the liver, exciting it to secretion when languid. Used with good effect in dyspepsia, diseases of the liver and spleen, and in the irritable condition of the stomach and bowels.

PREPARATIONS.

Fluid Extract of Dandelion.....................Dose, 1 to 2 Drams.
" " " " Compound.............. " 1 to 2 "
" " " " and Senna.............. " 1 to 2 "
Solid Extract................................ " 10 to 20 Grains.
Pills of Extract of Dandelion....................3 Grains each.

INFUSION OF DANDELION

Fluid Extract...............................Two Ounces.
Water.......................................One Pint.

Dose—Four to six ounces.

MIXTURE OF DANDELION.

Fluid Extract of Dandelion.....................Two Ounces.
" " " Peppermint.....................Two Ounces.
Clarified Honey..............................One Ounce.
Water.......................................Four Ounces.

Dose—Two to three drams.

PILLS OF DANDELION AND BLUE MASS.

Solid Extract of Dandelion................Five Scruples.
" " " Uva Ursi.......... .....Two-and-a-half Scruples.
Blue Mass.............................Ten Grains.

Mix, and form ten pills. One to be taken three times a day. In dropsy complicated with disease of the liver.

COMPOUND INFUSION OF DANDELION.

Fluid Extract of Dandelion................Six Drams.
" " " Rhubarb.................One-and-a-half Drams.
" " " Hyoscyamus.............Twenty-four Drops.
Carbonate of Soda.......... ....Half Dram.
Tartrate of Potassa.........................Three Drams.
Water ....Three-and-a-half Ounces.

One-third to be taken three times a day. In dropsical and visceral affections. *Dr. Meigs.*

COMPOUND PILLS OF DANDELION.

1.

Solid Extract of Dandelion......................One Ounce.
" " " Mandrake.....................One "
" " " Conium.......................One "

Mix, and divide into three-grain pills. Dose—Two or three. Valuable in hepatic and bilious affections.

2.

Solid Extract of Dandelion ....One Dram.
" " " Bloodroot.....................One Dram.
Podophyllin..................................Half Scruple.
Oil of Peppermint...........................Five Minims.

Mix, and divide into fifty pills. Dose—One to two, three times a day. Laxative, nauseant and diuretic; of much efficacy in jaundice, hepatic diseases, and affections of the kidneys.

3.

Solid Extract of Dandelion......................Three Drams.
Pulverized Nux Vomica.......................Two Scruples.
Sulphate of Alum...............................Ten Grains.

Mix, and divide into twenty pills, to be taken, one at night, and one at noon. In dyspepsia.

SYRUP OF DANDELION.

Fluid Extract of Dandelion........................Three Ounces.
Syrup..Thirteen Ounces.

Dose—Half to one ounce.

SYRUP DANDELION COMPOUND.

Fluid Extract Dandelion.......................Twelve Ounces.
" " Boneset.........................Two Ounces.
" " Ginger.........................Half Ounce.
Tincture of Cloves...........................Half Ounce.
Syrup...Five Ounces.
Brandy.......................................Eight Ounces.

Dose—Two to three drams. *J. Stevens.*

DANDELION COMPOUND.

Compounded of Dandelion, Mandrake, Conium.

TRIFOLIUM PRATENSE.

Red Clover.

A biennial plant, common in the United States. The blossoms are officinal.

MEDICAL PROPERTIES.

Highly recommended in cancerous ulcers of every kind, and deep, ragged-edged, and otherwise badly conditioned burns.

PREPARATION.

Solid Extract.............................To be used at discretion.

OINTMENT OF RED CLOVER.

Solid Extract..................................Four Ounces.
Lard..Half Pound.

TRILLIUM PENDULUM.

Bethroot.

Common in the Middle and Western States, growing in rich soils, in damp, rocky and shady woods. The root is the part used in medicine.

MEDICAL PROPERTIES.

Astringent, tonic and antiseptic. It has been employed successfully in hematuria, leucorrhea, cough, asthma, and difficult breathing.

PREPARATIONS.

Fluid Extract.................................Dose, 1 to 3 Drams.
Trilliin.......... .... " 4 to 8 Grains.

INFUSION OF BETHROOT.

Fluid Extract...............................Two Ounces.
Water.......................................One Pint.
Dose—Two to four ounces.

VALERIANA OFFICINALIS.

Valerian.

The Valerian is a European plant, flowering in June or July. The root is officinal.

MEDICAL PROPERTIES.

Valerian is tonic and antispasmodic. It is useful in cases of irregular nervous action, in the morbid vigilance of fevers, in hypochondriasis, epilepsy, and occasionally in intermittent and remittent fevers.

PREPARATIONS.

Fluid Extract.............................Dose, 1-2 to 1 1-2 Drams.
Solid Extract.............................. " 3 to 10 Grains.
Pills.....................................2 Grains each.

TINCTURE OF VALERIAN.

Fluid Extract...............................Eight Ounces.
Diluted Alcohol.............................Two Pints.
Dose—Two to four drams.

INFUSION OF VALERIAN.

Fluid Extract...............................Half Ounce.
Water.......................................One Pint.
Dose—Two to four ounces.

SYRUP OF VALERIAN.

Fluid Extract...............................Four Ounces.
Syrup.......................................One Pint.
Dose—Two to four drams.

WINE OF VALERIAN.

Fluid Extract..................................Two Ounces.
Sherry Wine..................................Fourteen Ounces.
Dose—Half to one ounce.

COMPOUND INFUSION OF VALERIAN.

Fluid Extract of Valerian..................One-and-a-half Ounces.
Syrup of Chamomile.........................One-and-a-half Ounces.
Camphor...................................Twenty Grains.
Infusion of Cinchona.......................Two Pints.
Dose—One to two ounces, three times a day. *Saunders.*

AMMONIATED TINCTURE OF VALERIAN.

Fluid Extract..................................Four Ounces.
Aromatic Spirit of Ammonia....................Two Pints.
Dose—One to two drams.

VALERIAN COMPOUND.

Fluid Extract of Valerian......................Two Ounces.
" " " Cinchona......................Half Ounce.
Carbonate of Ammonia.........................Two Drams.
Syrup of Ginger...............................One Ounce.
Dose—Two drams every hour in periodic hemicrania.
Donald Monro.

COMPOUND TINCTURE OF VALERIAN.

Fluid Extract of Valerian......................Two Ounces.
Tincture of Castor.............................One Ounce.
Fluid Extract of Saffron.......................One Ounce.
" " " Peppermint.....................Four Ounces.
Diluted Alcohol...............................Two Pints.
Dose—Half to one-and-a-half drams. *Wirt. Ph.*

VERATRUM VIRIDE.

American Hellebore.

This plant is indigenous to many parts of the United States, usually growing in swamps, wet meadows, and on the banks of mountain streamlets. The rhizoma is the officinal part.

MEDICAL PROPERTIES.

It is slightly acrid, an excellent expectorant, a certain diaphoretic, nervine, and never narcotic, emetic, and arterial sedative, which last is its most valuable and interesting property, and for which it stands unparalleled and unequalled as a therapeutic agent.

PREPARATIONS.

Fluid Extract...Dose :—

Each fluid ounce represents one ounce of crude root, and calculating 60 minims, or 120 drops to the fluid dram, each grain is represented by one minim, or two drops; therefore, for an adult male, begin with two drops, increasing one drop each portion given, or, for greater convenience or certainty of administration, combine in equal proportions with simple syrup, or syrup of squills, and give 4 drops, increasing 1 or 2 drops each portion, till nausea or vomiting ensues, or the pulse is reduced to 65 or 70 beats per minute. For children, begin with 1 drop of Veratrum, combined with equal portions of syrup of squills, and increase 1 drop each portion. When the pulse is sufficiently diminished, then reduce the dose one half—in all cases continuing it a sufficient length of time to prevent any return of the symptoms. Morphine or laudanum with brandy is a perfect antidote for an overdose of Veratrum; or syrup of sulphate of morphine one part, fluid extract of ginger two parts. Dose of this mixture for an adult male, 60 drops every 15 minutes till relieved.

Veratrin.......................................Dose, 1-16 to 1-2 Grain.

Pills ....1-2 and 1-4 Grain each.

INFUSION OF VERATRUM.

Fluid Extract...................................One Dram.

Water...Eight Ounces.

Dose—Two to four drams each hour. The doses should be too small to produce emesis. *T. C. Miller.*

WINE OF VERATRUM.

Fluid Extract...................................Four Ounces.

Sherry Wine....................................One Pint.

Dose—Twenty to forty drops.

XANTHOXYLUM FRAXINEUM.

Prickly Ash.

This species is indigenous. The leaves and capsules have an aromatic odor. The bark is the officinal portion.

MEDICAL PROPERTIES.

It is a stimulant, tonic and alterative. Used in languid conditions of the system; in rheumatism, chronic syphilis and hepatic derangements. The Xanthoxylin may be used in all cases when it is desired to stimulate and strengthen mucous tissues. A valuable tonic in low typhoid fever.

PREPARATIONS.

Fluid Extract..........Dose, 15 to 45 Drops.
Xanthoxylin..........“ 2 to 6 Grains.
Pills..........1 Grain each.

TINCTURE OF PRICKLY ASH.

Fluid Extract..........Four Ounces.
Diluted Alcohol..........One Pint.

Dose—Half to one-and-a-half drams.

INFUSION OF PRICKLY ASH.

Fluid Extract..........One Ounce.
Water..........One Quart.

One pint to be taken in divided doses during the 24 hours; in chronic rheumatism.

CLYSTER OF PRICKLY ASH.

Fluid Extract of Prickly Ash..........Two Ounces.
“ “ “ Opium..........Five Drams.
Water..........One Pint.

Xanthoxylin.......... One Dram.
Cimicifugin.......... “ “
Apocynin.......... “ “
Proof Spirit..........One Pint.

Dose—Four drams three times a day in chronic rheumatism.

Xanthoxylin..........Six Grains
Hydrastin.......... “ “

Dose—Three grains. Stimulating tonic for children, after diarrhea, dysentery, and other debilitating diseases.

ZINGIBER OFFICINALE.

Ginger.

This plant is a native of Hindustan, and is cultivated in all parts of India. The flowers have an aromatic smell, and the bruised stems are slightly fragrant; but the root is the portion in which the virtues of the plant reside. The Jamaica ginger is considered the best, and is mainly in use.

MEDICAL PROPERTIES.

Ginger is a grateful stimulant and carminative, often given in dyspepsia, flatulency, and imperfect digestion, as well as in colic, nausea, gout, spasms, cholera-morbus, &c. It is an excellent addition to bitter infusions and the like.

PREPARATION.

Fluid Extract............................ ...Dose, 1-2 to 1 1-2 Drams.

TINCTURE OF GINGER.

Fluid Extract ....Four Ounces.
Diluted Alcohol..............................Twelve Ounces.

Dose—Two to four drams.

INFUSION OF GINGER.

Fluid Extract................................One Ounce
Water..One Pint.

Dose—One to two ounces.

SYRUP OF GINGER.

Fluid Extract................................Two Ounces.
Syrup..One Pint.

Dose—One to two drams.

MISCELLANEOUS FORMULÆ.

INFUSIONS.

TONIC INFUSION.

Infusion of Cinchona........................Two-and-a-half Ounces.
" " Gentian Compound..............One Ounce.
Tincture of Cascarilla........................Two Drams.
Solution of Sesquicarb. Potassa..............Two Drams.

Dose—One ounce twice a day. *Pearson.*

IN GASTRALGIA.

Fluid Extract of Opium Aqueous ....Two Drams.
" " " Aconite........................Three Drams.
Distilled Water...............................Four Ounces.

Dose—One to two drams. twice a day, immediately after a meal.
Padiolcan

VERMIFUGE INFUSION.

Corsican Moss...............................Half Ounce.
Boiling Milk..................................Two Ounces.
Infuse, strain, and add :
Syrup of Wormwood..........................Ten Drams.

To be taken in one or two portions in the morning, fasting, for three days running, in the treatment of ascarides lumbricoides. The third day, from two-and-a-half drams to half ounce of castor oil to be given an hour after the administration of the vermifuge milk. *T. & R.*

ALKALINE INFUSION.

Hickory Ashes ....One Pint
Wood Soot ....Four Ounces.
Boiling Water..............................Half Gallon.

Let them stand twenty-four hours, and decant. Dose—A wineglassful three or four times a day, in lithiasis and dyspepsia. (This was a favorite remedy of Dr. Physick.)

IN TUBERCULOSIS.

Citrate of Iron .... Two Scruples.
Syrup of Orange Peel.................. .... One Ounce.
Tincture of Cardamom Compound................ One Ounce.
Infusion of Colombo............................ Four Ounces.

Dose—One ounce thrice a day. *H. Bennett.*

A SPECIFIC IN APTHÆ.

Fluid Extract of Ipecac .... Fifteen Drops.
" " " Opium, Aqueous............... Five "
" " " Spearmint.................... Ten "
Water.. Twenty-four Drams.

Dose—One dram every two hours; at the same time apply to the tongue equal parts of borax and loaf sugar.

COMPOUND SQUILL INFUSION.

Flaxseed (bruised)............................ One Ounce.
White Mustard (bruised)...................... Half Ounce.
Fluid Ext. Squill.............................. One Dram.
Carbonate of Soda............................. One Dram.
Water... One Pint.

Dose—Four to six ounces, every two to four hours. *M. & D.*

COMPOUND BITTER INFUSION.

Fluid Ext. Colombo............................ Two Drams.
" " Quassia............................ Two Drams.
" " Orange Peel......................... One Dram.
" " Rhubarb............................ Half "
Carbonate of Potassa........................... " "
Spirits Lavender Compound..................... Half Ounce.
Water... One Pint.

Dose—Two ounces, thrice a day.

This is an excellent form for exhibiting a tonic in convalescence from fever. *M. & D.*

DIURETIC AND TONIC INFUSION.

Fluid Extract of Colombo...................... Two Drams.
" " " Ginger........................ " "
" " " Squill......................... " "
Bitartrate of Potassa.......................... Four "
Water.. One-and-a-half Pints.

Dose—Two ounces, three times a day. *Baillie.*

MIXTURES.

IN DROPSICAL AFFECTIONS.

Fluid Extract of Squill..........................Half Ounce.
" " " Opium..........................Two Drams.
Essence of Cinnamon..........................Two Drams.

Dose—Half to one dram, twice a day. *Paris.*

IN DIARRHEA AND DYSENTERY.

Dover's Powder..........................Five Grains.
Chalk Mixture..........................Twelve Drams.
Spirits of Cinnamon..........................Two Drams.
Syrup of Poppy..........................One Dram.

This draught to be taken every four hours, or after each liquid motion. *Hooper.*

ANTI-DYSENTERIC MIXTURE.

Fluid Extract of Rhubarb..........................Two Drams.
" " " Ipecac..........................One Dram.
" " " Canella..........................One Dram.

Dose—Half dram every three hours. *M. & D.*

IN DYSPEPSIA.

Solution of Carbonate of Potassa..........................Half Dram.
Infusion of Gentian Compound..........................Half Ounce.
Tincture of Cascarilla..........................One Dram.

One draft. To be taken occasionally. *Duncan.*

IN DYSPEPSIA.

Solution of Carbonate of Potassa..........................Twenty Minims.
Chalk Mixture..........................Two Ounces.
Tincture of Colombo..........................Two Ounces.

Dose—A teasponful in water, three times a day. *Frank.*

IN ACIDITY OF THE PRIMÆ VIÆ.

Water of Ammonia..........................Sixteen Minims.
Almond Mixture..........................Two Ounces.
Fluid Ext. Opium (Aqueous)..........................Ten Minims.

Make a draught. To be taken three times a day. *A. T. Thompson.*

10

IN CARDIALGIA AND FLATULENCE IN GOUTY HABITS.

Infusion of Colombo .... Six Ounces.
Tincture of Colombo .... One Dram.
Carbonate of Ammonia .... Half Dram.

Dose—One-and-a-half ounces, morning and noon. *Brande.*

IN TYPHUS, &c.

Infusion of Cinchona .... Six Ounces.
Tincture of Cinchona Compound .... One Ounce.
Diluted Sulphuric Acid .... One Dram.
Syrup of Orange Peel .... Half Ounce.

Dose—Two ounces every two hours. *Lomnius*

ANTI-SPASMODIC MIXTURE IN LARYNGISMUS STRIDULUS.

Fetid Spirit of Ammonia .... Half Dram.
Tincture of Hyoscyamus .... Ten Drops.
Syrup of Orange Peel .... Half Ounce.
Spirit of Anise .... One Dram.
Diluted Hydrocyanic Acid .... Five Drops.
Water .... One Ounce.

Dose—One dram, three times a day, for an infant ten or twelve months old; the dose to be graduated according to age. *Reid.*

IN THE EARLY STAGES OF UNCOMPLICATED HOOPING COUGH.

Syrup of Poppy .... One Dram.
Sulphate of Magnesia .... One Dram.
Camphor Mixture .... One-and-a-half Ounces.

Dose—The fourth part every three hours. *R. Williams.*

DEWEE'S COLCHICUM MIXTURE

Wine of Colchicum Seed .... Thirty Drops.
Denarcotized Laudanum .... Twenty-five Drops.
Sugar .... Thirty Grains.
Water .... One Ounce.

To be taken at night, in one draught. *P.*

SCUDAMORE'S MIXTURE FOR GOUT.

Sulphate of Magnesia .... One Ounce.
Mint Water .... Ten Ounces.
Vinegar of Colchicum .... One Ounce.
Syrup of Saffron .... One Ounce.
Magnesia .... Two-and-two-thirds Drams.

Mix. Dose—One to three tablespoonfuls every two hours, till four to six evacuations are procured in the twenty-four hours. *P.*

PURGING DRAUGHT.

Gamboge.................................Five Grains.
Tincture of Senna Compound..................One Dram.
" " Jalap..........................One Dram.
Infusion of Senna Compound..................One Ounce.

Knighton.

IN ICTERUS.

Infusion of Cinchona........................Ten Drams.
Tincture of Colombo..........................Two Drams.
Carbonate of Potassa........................Twelve Grains.

Make a draught. To be taken in the morning, and one hour before dinner, on an empty stomach. *Hamilton.*

IN ANASARCA ; DIURETIC AND TONIC.

Infusion of Gentian Compound ....Five Ounces.
Acetate of Potassa.............................Half Dram.
Spirits of Juniper Compound....................Half Ounce.
Compound Spirit of Horse Radish................Half Ounce.
Spirits of Nitric Ether.........................Two Drams.

Make a mixture. *F.*

IN PHOSPHATIC DEPOSITS FROM THE URINE.

Diluted Phosphoric Acid.........................One Ounce.
Infusion of Colombo.............................Fourteen Ounces.
Tincture of Cardamon Compound..................One Ounce.

Dose—One ounce, three times a day. *F.*

IN PROTRACTED DYSENTERY.

Fluid Extract of Logwood.......................Five Drams.
Spirits of Cinnamon............................One Ounce.
Tincture of Catechu............................Two Drams.
Water. ....Seven Ounces.

Dose—One ounce, every five hours. *Pringle.*

IN DYSPEPTIC CONSTIPATION.

Infusion of Senna Compound.....................One Ounce.
Tincture " " " ....One Dram.
" " Jalap.............................. " "
Syrup of Senna. .... " "
Tartrate of Potassa............................ " "

Make a draught. To be taken early in the morning. *Currie.*

CATHARTIC DRAUGHT.

Infusion of Senna Compound................One-and-a-half Ounces.
Tincture of Jalap..........................One Dram.
" " Castor.... ....One Dram.
Fluid Extract of Aqueous Opium............Ten Minims.
Sulphate of Magnesia......................Six Drams.

Paris.

IN PALPITATION OF THE HEART FROM NERVOUS IRRITABILITY.

Tincture of Digitalis.........................Twenty Minims.
" " Colombo..........................One Dram.
Camphor Mixture..............................Ten Drams.
Make a draught. One, twice a day. *Paris.*

IN HOOPING COUGH.

Fluid Ext. Opium (Aqueous)...................Fifteen Minims.
Wine of Ipecac...............................One Dram.
Carbonate of Soda............................Twenty-four Grains.
Syrup..Three Drams.
Water............ .... One Ounce.
A sixth part every four or six hours, for a child. *Pearson.*

LAXATIVE MIXTURE.

Sulphate of Magnesia..........................One Ounce.
Manna...Two Drams.
Infusion of Senna Compound...................Six "
Tincture " " " ....Two "
Infusion of Spearmint.........................One Ounce.
Distilled Water...............................Two Ounces.
Dose—One-and-a-half ounces, night and morning. *Abernethy.*

APERIENT DRAUGHT.

Infusion of Senna Compound ....Twelve Drams.
Syrup of Orange Peel..........................One Dram.
Sulphate of Magnesia... ....Six Drams.

Blundell.

ANTI-HYSTERIC DRAUGHT.

Fluid Extract of Valerian.............. ....Half Dram.
Tincture of Ammoniated Valerian...............One Dram.
Tincture of Castor............................One Dram.
Camphor Mixture...............................Twelve Drams.
To be taken three times a day. *Frank.*

AROMATIC APERIENT DRAUGHT.

Infusion of Senna Compound................One-and-a-half Ounces.
Tincture of Rhubarb " ....Two Drams.
" " Lavender " ....One Dram.

F.

IN HOOPING COUGH.

Fluid Extract of Conium ....Five Drops.
Infusion of Cinchona.........................One Ounce.
Fluid Extract of Opium (Aqueous)..............Five Minims.

Make a draught. One, three times a day. *Webster.*

IN ASTHMA, FROM DISEASE OF THE HEART.

Tincture of Lobelia...............................Two Drams.
" " Hyoscyamus......................Three Drams.
" " Digitalis ....Twenty Minims.
Compound Spirits of Ether ....Three Drams.
Camphor Mixture ....Five-and-a-half Ounces.

Dose—A tablespoonful occasionally, or during the fit. *F.*

IN HYSTERIA.

Fluid Extract of Cinchona......................One Ounce.
" " " Valerian.....................Two Drams.
Syrup ....Five Drams.

Dose—One dram occasionally. *Frank.*

COMPOUND MIXTURE OF GENTIAN.

Compound Infusion of Gentian ....Twelve Ounces.
" " " Senna...................Six "
" Tincture of Cardamom ....Two "

Dose—One to two ounces. A tonic and cathartic preparation, adapted to dyspepsia and constipation.

SOOTHING JULEP.

Syrup of Extract of Opium........................Two Ounces.
" " Tolu.................................One Ounce.
Orange Flower Water...........................Six Drams.
Distilled Lettuce Water.........................Four Ounces.

To be made *secundum artem*, and taken by a tablespoonful at a time, from hour to hour. *T. & R.*

MIXTURE AGAINST CHILBLAINS.

Balsam of Peru..............................Half Ounce.
Dissolve it in Alcohol ....Four Ounces.

Add:

Hydrochloric Acid........... ....One Dram.
Tincture of Benzoin..........................Half Ounce.

To be rubbed upon the affected part several times a day. To be kept in a blue or black bottle, and labelled "For external use." *T. & R.*

PILLS.

ANTACID PILLS.

Solid Extract of Rhubarb......................One Scruple.
Carbonate of Soda............................ " "
Solid Extract of Gentian...................... " "
Calomel......................................Three Grains.

To be made into twenty pills. Dose—Two occasionally. In dyspepsia, with acidity of the stomach. *R.*

DR. KITCHENER'S PERISTALTIC PERSUADERS.

Solid Extract of Rhubarb..................One-and-a-half Drams.
Oil of Caraway............................Ten Minims.
Syrup.....................................Sufficient.

Divide into forty pills. Dose—Two to three pills.

A favorite aperient and carminative in CONSTIPATION and indigestion

ERGOT PILLS.

Pulverized Ergot.... ....Nine, Twelve or Eighteen Grains.
Solid Extract of Hyoscyamus...................One Grain.
Nitrate of Potassa.............................Fifteen Grains.
Pulverized Camphor..........................Three Grains.
Excipient...................................Sufficient.

Mix, and divide into forty pills. *D.*

COMPOUND PILLS OF IODIDE OF MERCURY.

Iodide of Mercury.............................Ten Grains.
Resin of Guaiacum............................Two Scruples.
Solid Extract of Conium.................... .Fifteen Grains.

Triturate the resin of guaiacum into a mass with a little alcohol, then incorporate with it the extract of conium and iodide of mercury, and divide into twenty pills.

These pills are alterative, and may be used in scrofulous and skin diseases. Extract of Sarsaparilla may be added to, or substituted for some of the other ingredients. *P.*

DR. CHAPMAN'S DINNER PILLS.

Powdered Aloes..............................Eighteen Grains.
" Mastich.............................. " "
" Ipecac..............................Twelve "
Oil of Caraway..............................Two Minims.

Mix, and make twelve pills. Dose—One before dinner. *P.*

MITCHELL'S APERIENT PILLS.

Powdered Aloes..............................Twelve Grains.
" Rhubarb..............................Twenty-four "
Calomel..............................Two
Tart. Antim. and Potassa..............................One Grain.

Mix, and make pills No. 12. One acts as an aperient; two or three as a cathartic. *P.*

IN HYDROTHORAX AND ASCITES.

Solid Ext. Digitalis..............................Six Grains.
Calomel..............................Six "
Powdered Opium..............................Four "
Confection of Rose..............................Sufficient.

Make twelve pills. One to be taken every eight hours. *E.*

IN DROPSY COMPLICATED WITH DISEASE OF THE LIVER.

Solid Ext. Dandelion..............................One Dram.
" " Uva Ursi..............................One Dram.
Calomel..............................Ten Grains.

Make ten pills. Two to be taken morning, noon and night. *E.*

IN DROPSY.

Solid Ext. Digitalis..............................Six Grains.
" " Gentian..............................Half Dram.
Powdered Squill..............................Half Dram.
Oil of Juniper..............................Eight Drops.
Syrup..............................Sufficient.

Make twelve pills. Dose—One, three times, daily. *Pearson.*

ALTERATIVE AND DIURETIC IN ANASARCA.

Solid Ext. Digitalis..............................Five Grains.
Powdered Squill..............................Ten Grains.
Blue Mass..............................Half Dram.
Syrup of Acacia..............................Sufficient.

Make ten pills. Dose—One, three times, daily. *Baillie.*

RHUBARB AND SULPHATE OF IRON.

Solid Extract of Rhubarb....................One-and-a-half Drams.
Sulphate of Iron............................Half Dram.
Soap..Two Scruples.
Distilled Water.......................Sufficient.

Mix, and divide into forty pills.

ALTERATIVES, IN DERANGEMENT OF THE LIVER.

Blue Mass..................................Nine Grains.
Solid Ext. Rhubarb...........................Twenty-four Grains.
Bicarbonate of Soda.........................Twelve Grains.
Syrup of Rhubarb, Aromatic..................Sufficient.

Make into twelve pills. Dose—One, two or three times a day.

Dr. Hartshorne.

PILLS OF BLUE MASS AND COLOCYNTH.

Blue Mass..................................Five Grains.
Solid Ext. Colocynth Compound................Five Grains.
Oil of Caraway ....Two Drops.

Mix, and make two pills. These constitute an active cathartic. *E.*

ANTI-GOUT PILL.

Acetic Extract of Colchicum................Ten Grains.
Solid Ext. Colocynth Compound.............Ten Grains.
Muriate of Morphia.........................Two-and-a-half Grains.

Mix, and make ten pills. Dose—One pill should be given every two hours, until the bowels and kidneys are acted on. *Robert Dick.*

PILLS WITH BUTTERNUT AND JALAP.

Solid Extract of Butternut......................Half Dram.
" " " Jalap..........................One Scruple.
Soap.......................................Ten Grains.

Mix, and make twelve pills. Two or three of these may be taken at a dose and if they do not operate, two or more may be safely administered. The extract of butternut, either alone or in combination, is highly recommended as a cathartic in fevers, dysentery, &c.

ANTICEPHALGIC PILLS

Solid Extract of Belladonna................Ten Grains.
" " " Hyoscyamus...............Fifteen "
" " " Lettuce....................Twenty "
" " " Opium...................Three "
Butter of Cacao.............................One-and-a-half Drams.

Divide into sixty pills. Dose—One, night and morning. *Broussais.*

FOR NERVOUS HEADACHE.

Solid Ext. Rhubarb............................Half Dram.
" " Chamomile..........................One Scruple.
Nutmeg....................................Half Dram.
Oil of Peppermint............................Sufficient.

Divide into thirty pills. Dose—Three, twice a day. *Dr. Wilson.*

ANTI-EPILEPTIC PILLS.

Solid Ext. Belladonna..........................Six Grains.
Oxide of Zinc................................Nine "
Camphor ....Six "

Make twelve pills. One, three times a day. *Recamier.*

FOR CHRONIC INDIGESTION AND IRRITABILITY OF STOMACH.

Subnitrate of Bismuth..........................One Dram.
Solid Ext. Rhubarb............................Half "
Powdered Rhubarb, Aromatic...................Two Scruples.
Syrup ....Sufficient.

Make into eight pills. Take one before each meal. *P.*

PILLS OF CAMPHOR AND OPIUM.

Camphor ....Twenty-four Grains.
Powdered Opium...............................Six Grains.
Alcohol.....................................Six Drops.
Confection of Rose...........................Sufficient.

Mix, and make twelve pills. Dose—One to two. *P.*

LARTIGUE'S GOUT PILLS.

Solid Ext. Colocynth Compound.................Two Drams.
" " Digitalis..............................Ten Grains.
Acetic Ext. Colchicum.........................Ten Grains.

Make twenty-four pills. Dose—Two. *P.*

LAXATIVE TONIC PILLS. (Dr. Parrish, Senior.)

Powdered Socotrine Aloes......................Two Scruples.
Solid Ext. Rhubarb............................Four "
" " Gentian...........................Two "
Oil of Caraway...............................Twelve Drops.

Make into thirty pills. Dose—Two before dinner. *P.*

ANTI-NEURALGIC PILLS.

Solid Ext. Stramonium........................Eight Grains.
Extract of Opium (Aqueous)....................Eight Grains.
Oxide of Zinc ....Two Drams.
Excipient......................... ......Sufficient.

For forty pills. From one to eight may be taken in the course of twenty-four hours, and the dose should be pushed until the patient experiences hallucinations, or at any rate considerable disorder of vision. *T. & R.*

PILLS FOR CHRONIC CATARRH OF THE BRONCHI AND BLADDER.

Turpentine....................................Half Ounce.
Balsam of Tolu................................Half Dram.
Ammoniac..... ....One Dram.
Watery Extract of Opium.......................Six Grains.
Excipient.....................................Sufficient.

For seventy-eight pills. To take five daily. *T. & R.*

FERRUGINOUS PILLS.

Iron Filings, with a metallic lustre..............Half Ounce.
Soft Extract of Cinchona.......................Seventy-five Grains.
Some inert Excipient...........................Sufficient.

Mix them carefully, and divide the mass into 100 pills, which are to be rolled in powdered gum. From one to ten to be taken daily, during meals. Used in simple chlorosis, anæmia, and convalescence from intermitting fevers. *T. & R.*

FERRUGINOUS PILLS.

Iron reduced by hydrogen.......................Half Ounce.
Sub-nitrate of Bismuth.........................Five Drams.
Watery Extract of Opium........................Three Grains.
Syrup of Gum...................................Sufficient.

Mix, and divide into 125 pills. To be taken daily, during meals.

Used in chlorosis, with pain in the stomach (gastralgia), or in the bowels (enteralgia), or a tendency to diarrhea. *T. & R.*

TONIC FERRUGINOUS PILLS.

Iron reduced by hydrogen..................Two-and-a-half Drams.
Dry Extract of Cinchona...................Seventy-five Grains.
Powdered Rhubarb........................ " "
Syrup of Gum..............................Sufficient.

Mix, and divide into eighty pills. In chlorosis; anæmia, with constipation, and loss of power in the digestive canal.

ANTICHLOROTIC PILLS.

Iron Filings, porphyrized..........................One Dram.
Solid Ext. Wormwood..........................Sufficient.

Mix, and make thirty-six pills. Three or four to be taken night and morning.

IN HABITUAL CONSTIPATION.

Solid Ext. Hyoscyamus..........................Thirty Grains.
" " Colocynth..........................Twenty "
" " Nux Vomica..........................Three "

Make twenty-five pills. Dose—One, night and morning.

DR. MITCHELL'S TONIC PILLS.

Solid Ext. Quassia..........................Thirty-six Grains.
" " Conium..........................Three "
Subcarbonate of Iron..........................Three "

Make into a mass, with a few drops of solution of arsenite of potassa, (if required); then divide into twelve pills. Dose—One, twice or three times daily. *P.*

TONIC AND AROMATIC PILLS. (Dr. Parrish, Senior.)

Sulphate of Quinia..........................Three Grains.
Powdered Capsicum..........................Six "
Mace..........................Six "
Powdered Cloves..........................Six "
Carbonate of Ammonia..........................Six "
Oil of Caraway..........................Three Drops.
Confection of Rose..........................Sufficient.

Form a uniform tenacious mass, and divide into twelve pills. *P.*

IN OBSTINATE INTERMITTENTS. (Dr. Chapman.)

Sulphate of Copper..........................Three Grains.
Powdered Opium..........................Four "
" Gum Arabic..........................Eight "
Syrup..........................Sufficient.

Make a mass, and divide into twelve pills. Dose—One every three hours. *P.*

IN SCIRRHOUS PHLEGMON.

Solid Ext. Conium..........................Thirty Grains.
" " Cinchona..........................One Dram.

Make thirty pills. One, three times a day. *Rush.*

ANTI-CATARRHAL PILLS.

Sulphuret of Calcium ....Fifteen Grains.
Solid Ext. Aconite........................Twenty Grains.
Inert Excipient..................................Sufficient.

Mix, and divide into twenty pills. From one to four, to be taken daily, in chronic pulmonary catarrh. *T. & R.*

BECHIR (EXPECTORANT) PILLS.

Solid Ext. Digitalis..............................Fifteen Grains.
White Oxide of Antimony........................Half Dram.
Inert Excipient..................................Sufficient.

Make forty pills. From one to six to be taken daily by children. From four to twenty by adults. Used in cases of catarrh of the pulmonary capillaries, pulmonary apoplexy, and subacute apoplexy. *T. & R.*

IN OBSTINATE CARDIALGIA AND GOUTY HABITS.

Solid Extract of Gentian......................One-and-a-half Drams.
Carbonate of Ammonia ....One Dram.

Make twenty-four pills. Two, twice or thrice a day. *Brande.*

IN DYSPEPSIA AND FLATULENT ACIDITY.

Carbonate of Ammonia.........................Five Grains.
Solid Ext. Rhubarb............................Eight Grains.

Make three pills. *Paris*

HYDRAGOGUE PILLS.

Assafœtida ....Half Dram.
Powdered Squill.............................Half Dram.
Solid Ext. Colocynth..........................Fifteen Grains.
" " Digitalis .... Ten Grains.

Make twenty pills. Two every three hours, in symptomatic dropsies. *Bouchardat.*

ANODYNE PILLS.

Opium.......................................Four Grains.
Solid Ext. Hyoscyamus........................Six "
" " Conium............................Eight "

Make six pills. One each night. *Darwin.*

ANTI-EPILEPTIC PILLS.

Solid Extract of Belladonna.....................Four Grains.
Oxide of Zinc...................................Six Grains.

Make six pills. One, night and morning. *Recamier.*

TO PREVENT PRIAPISM OR CHORDEE IN ACUTE GONORRHEA, AND ALSO IN CHANCRES IN THE URETHRA.

Camphor.......................................Two Scruples.
Solid Ext. Lettuce..................................One Dram.

Make twenty pills. Two at bed-time. *Ricord.*

IN OBSTINATE GLEET.

Solid Ext. Nux Vomica.......................Twelve Grains.
Disulphate of Quinia.........................Twenty-four Grains.
Solid Ext. Hyoscyamus......................Twenty-four Grains.

Make twenty-four pills. Two to be taken one hour before each meal. *Johnson.*

IN DYSMENORRHEA.

Camphor.......................................One Scruple.
Solid Ext. Hop...............................One Dram.
" " Lettuce...............................One Scruple.

Make into twenty pills. Three when the pain commences, and occasionally afterwards. *Rigby.*

TO RELIEVE THE PAIN IN DYSMENORRHŒA.

Solid Ext. Hyoscyamus.......................Two Grains.
Camphor.......................................Three Grains.
Powdered Ipecac..............................One Grain.

Make two pills. To be taken two or three times a day. *Ashwell.*

POWDERS.

IN DIARRHEA FROM ACIDITY.

Compound Powder of Chalk with Opium..........One Scruple.
Powder of Catechu Extr.......................Fifteen Grains.

Make powder. One to be taken after each liquid motion. *Paris.*

ALLEN'S ANTI-DYSENTERIC.

Precipitated Carbonate of Lime.................Two Drams.
Dover's Powder...............................One Scruple.
Powdered Rhubarb.............................One Dram.
Gum Opium....................................Two Grains.

Make four powders. Dose—One, night and morning, in syrup. *M. & D.*

IN OBSTINATE CONSTIPATION IN TRAUMATIC TETANUS.

Powdered Scammony.......................Half Dram.
" Jalap.......................One Dram.
" Gamboge.......................Twelve Grains.
" Ginger.......................Ten Grains.

Make three powders. Dose—One, every three hours until the bowels act freely. *Bullen.*

EXPECTORANT POWDER.

Powdered Ipecac.......................Twelve Grains.
" Squill.......................Six "
Nitrate of Potassa.......................Thirty "

Make six powders. Dose—One, every four hours. *F.*

IN CALCULUS.

Powdered Uva Ursi.......................One Ounce.
Bicarbonate of Potassa.......................Half Ounce.

Dose—Twenty grains to one dram, twice or thrice daily. *Burns.*

IN REMITTING AND INTERMITTING FEVERS.

Powdered Cinchona.......................Half Dram.
" Cascarilla.......................Half Scruple.

Make a powder. To be taken frequently. *Hartmann.*

ARTERIAL SEDATIVE.

Tartrate of Antimony and Potassa.......................One Grain.
Nitrate of Potassa.......................Half Dram.
Sugar.......................Half Dram.

Triturate into powder, and distribute equally into twelve papers. *P.*

FOR THE DIARRHEA OF YOUNG CHILDREN.

Acetate of Lead.......................Two Grains.
Opium.......................Half Grain.
Camphor.......................One Grain.
Sugar.......................Three Grains.

Triturate, and divide into twelve papers. Dose—One, every two or three hours.

The child should be kept quiet, and fed upon arrowroot, flour boiled in milk, or a mixture of barley-water and cream.

For adults, the whole quantity prescribed may be taken at one dose. *P.*

DR. OTTO'S ANTI-SPASMODIC POWDERS.

Black Mustard Seed....................................One Ounce.
Powdered Sage....................................." "
" Ginger.."

Mix thoroughly.

Dose—Three teaspoonfuls, for three mornings in succession; discontinue three; then give as before. To be moistened with water or molasses.

This powder is highly recommended, in epilepsy, by several practitioners, and recently by Dr. Charles O. Hendry, of Haddonfield, N. J. *P.*

PURGATIVE POWDERS.

1.

Calomel..Five Grains.
Powdered Rhubarb.................................Five Grains.
Oil of Cinnamon..................................One Drop.

To be given in molasses. *E.*

2.

Calomel..Five Grains.
Powdered Jalap...................................Five "
" Rhubarb.......................................Five "
Oil of Cinnamon..................................One Drop.

To be given as the former. *E.*

3.

Compound Powder of Jalap.........................Three Drams.
Powdered Gamboge.................................Six Grains.

Divide into six papers. Dose—One powder, every two hours, in molasses or syrup. *E.*

FERRUGINOUS POWDERS.

Iron reduced by Hydrogen.........................Two Drams.
Powdered Sugar...................................Five Drams.

Mix them carefully, and divide the mixture into twenty equal packets. From one to four to be taken daily, in the first spoonful of soup, or in biscuit water.

Used in anæmia, and after hemorrhages and intermittent fevers.

T. & R.

IN SYCHOSIS MENTI.

Sulphate of Iron.................................Ten Parts.
Charcoal...Thirty-five Parts.

Mix. Used externally. *Dauvergne.*

STOMACHIC TONIC POWDERS.

Iron reduced by Hydrogen.... ....One Dram.
Powdered Gentian ....Half "
" Cinnamon...........................Half "
Calcined Magnesia...........................Half "

Mix them accurately, and divide into twenty packets. Dose—One to be taken night and morning, during a meal.

Used in pyrosis, and atony of the digestive canal. *T. & R.*

ANTI-NEURALGIC TONIC POWDERS.

Carbonate of Iron........................One-and-a-half Ounces.
Powdered Valerian Root..................Two-and-a-half Drams.

Mix, and divide into fifty packets. From one to ten to be taken daily.

Used in obstinate neuralgia of the temporo-facial nerves, accompanied with chlorosis. *T. & R.*

RESTORATIVE TONIC POWDERS.

Iron reduced by Hydrogen.................Two-and-a-half Drams.
Dry Extract of Cinchona..................Half Dram.

Mix, and divide into twenty packets. One to four to be taken daily.

Used in anæmia, and at the close of intermittent fevers. *T. & R.*

IN OBSTINATE DIARRHEAS AND PASSIVE HEMORRHAGES.

Alum ....One Dram.
Sugar....................................One Dram.
Opium ....Four Grains.

Mix for twelve powders. Dose—Two or three, daily.

Bouchardat.

IN HOOPING COUGH.

Belladonna..............................One to three Grains.
Musk....................................Five Grains.
Camphor................................. " "
White Sugar.............................Half Dram.

Mix for eight powders. *Kopp.*

OR,

Belladonna..... ....Two Grains.
Ipecac.................................... " "
Sulphur..... ....Thirty-two Grains.
Sugar of Milk............ .... " "

Mix for eight powders. Dose—Three, daily.

IN NEPHRITIC COMPLAINTS.

Powdered Uva Ursi........................One-and-a-half Drams.
Bicarbonate of Soda........................One Dram.

Make twelve powders. Dose—One, three times a day, to be taken in sugar and water. *R.*

SYRUPS.

BOULLAY'S SYRUP.

Fluid Extract of Ipecac.................. .....Two Drams.
" " " Cinchona......................One Ounce.
" " " Opium........................One Dram.
Syrup......................................Six Ounces.

Dose—One dram to half ounce, frequently, according to the age of the patient. Used in pertussis.

BALSAMIC SYRUP.

Venice Turpentine..........................Six-and-a-half Ounces.
Simple Syrup..............................Thirty-two Ounces.

Digest them in a water bath for twenty-four hours, strain, and add:

Rectified Oil of Turpentine.................. ....Thirty Drops.

Dose—One to six ounces, to be taken daily in chronic catarrh of the kidneys, of the bladder, or of the lungs; and in patients weakened by excessive suppuration. *T. & R.*

IN SCROFULOUS AFFECTIONS, ACCOMPANIED BY CHLOROSIS.

Tartrate of Potash and Iron ....Two-and-a-half Ounces.
Iodide of Potassium........................Two-and-a-half "
Cinnamon ....Two-and-a-half "
Water ....Two Ounces.
Simple Syrup..............................Sixteen Ounces.

Dissolve the salts in the filtered water; add the syrup, and shake them together. Dose—One to three ounces daily. *Mialhe.*

SYRUP OF SULPHATE OF STRYCHNINE.

Sulphate of Strychnine........................Four Grains.
Simple Syrup ....Sixteen Ounces.

Dissolve the sulphate of strychnine in a little water, and add the syrup. Shake them together. This syrup is employed in doses of from three to four teaspoonfuls to even six to eight tablespoonfuls in the course of the day, for children and young people affected with chorea, (St. Vitus' dance,) so as to produce considerable stiffness of the limbs, and a kind of tetanic twitchings. It is employed in paralysis in the same away. *T. & R.*

TINCTURES.

LIQUID SUBSTITUTE FOR DOVER'S POWDER.

Wine of Ipecac................................Sixteen Minims.
Tincture of Opium.............................Thirteen "
Spirit Nitric Ether...........................One Dram.

Take at one dose at going to bed. *P.*

A BITTER TONIC FOR DYSPEPSIA.

Tincture of Cinchona and Quassia Compound......Fourteen Ounces.
" " Nux Vomica.......................One Dram.

Dose—A teaspoonful three times a day in a little sugar and water. *P.*

IN DYSPEPSIA WITH ACIDITY.

Fluid Extract of Colombo......................One Ounce.
" " " Rhubarb.......................Half Ounce
" " " Ginger........................One Dram.
Dried Carbonate of Soda.......................Two Drams.
Diluted Alcohol...............................Four Ounces.
Dose—One to two drams. *R.*

CHEYNE'S STOMACHIC TINCTURE.

Fluid Extract of Rhubarb......................Two Ounces.
" " " Cinchona......................One Ounce.
" " " Orange Peel...................Half Ounce.
" " " Ginger........................Three Drams.
Compound Spirit of Juniper....................Two "
" Tincture of Cardamom................Two "
Sherry Wine...................................Two Pints.

Dose—Half to one ounce, twice or thrice a day. This was a favorite tincture of Dr. Cheyne, which he facetiously named *The Bishop.*

M. & D.

IN THE NERVOUS IRRITABILITY AND SLEEPLESSNESS OF DRUNKARDS.

Tincture of Colombo...........................One Ounce.
" " Quassia...........................". "
" " Gentian...........................". "
" " Cinchona..........................". "
Hydrochlorate of Morphia......................Two Grains.
Dose—One dram, three or four times a day—one hour before a meal.

Graves.

NARCOTIC MIXTURE.

Tincture of Belladonna........................Ten Drams.
Fl. Ext. Opium (Aqueous)....................Ten Drams.

Mix. Used by means of friction, or poured upon the face of a poultice to the extent of one or two tablespoonfuls, to allay pain. *T. & R.*

AS PROPHYLACTIC OF CHOLERA.

Tincture of Aconite........................Three Drams.
Fluid Extract of Aqueous Opium............One-and-a-half Drams.
Extract of Aloes.........................One Dram.

Dose—Ten drops, to be taken every morning in a spoonful of Madeira or coffee. *Franceschi.*

RECOMMENDED IN CHOLERA.

Etherial Tincture of Valerian...................One Ounce.
Tincture of Nux Vomica............ ....Half "
Spirit of Sulphuric Ether......................One "
Tincture of Arnica.............................Half "
Fluid Ext. Aqueous Opium....................Six Drams.
" " Peppermint ....Two Drams.

Dose—Twenty to forty drops in a little peppermint infusion, given frequently.

FOX'S TINCTURE.

Infusion of Horse-Radish ....Four Ounces.
Fluid Extract of Valerian ....Two Drams.
" " " Rhubarb ....Half Ounce
Sherry Wine...............................Two Pints.

Dose—One ounce every three hours. Used in paralysis and chronic rheumatism.

IN MENSTRUAL RETENTION.

Tincture of Aloes Compound...............One-and-a-half Ounces.
" " Black Hellebore................Two Drams.
" " Castor.......................Two Drams.
" " Cantharides...................Half Dram.

Dose—Half to one-and-a-half drams. *Clarke.*

IN BRONCHITIS WITH TENDENCY TO ASTHMA.

Tincture of Lobelia...........................Half Ounce.
" " Opium, Camphorated................Half "
" " Bloodroot ....One "
Empyreumatic Syrup.........................Six Ounces.

Dose—Half to one dram, several times a day. *F.*

LITHONTRIPTIC TINCTURE.

Fluid Ext. Gentian Compound....................Two Ounces.
" " " Ginger....................One Ounce.
" " " Spearmint....................One Ounce.
Bicarbonate of Potassa....................Two Drams.
Diluted Alcohol....................Six Ounces.

Dose—Two to four drams three times a day.

PEYRILKE'S ELIXIR.

Fluid Extract of Gentian....................Half Ounce.
Carbonate of Potassa....................One Dram.
Diluted Alcohol....................One Pint.

Dose—Half ounce three times a day. With this Elixir, Mons. Peyrilke obtained great reputation in the treatment of scrofula.

WINES.

ANTI-GOUT WINE OF DR. ANDERSON.

Fluid Extract of Colchicum Root....................Thirty Parts.
Leaves of the Ash Tree....................Thirty "
Tincture of Aconite....................Eight "
" " Digitalis....................Five "
Malaga Wine....................Five Hundred parts.

Dose—One dram morning and evening in a cup of tea, for gout and articular rheumatism.

RADCLIFFE'S WINE.

White Mustard....................Three Drams.
Gentian Root....................One Dram.
Coriander Seed....................One-and-a-half Drams.
Pulverized Nutmeg....................One-and-a-half Drams.
Sherry Wine....................Two Pints.

Digest for five days, and filter for use.

This wine was much used by the celebrated Dr. Radcliffe, and was by him believed to be particularly adapted to support the vis vitæ, when the constitution had been impaired by the intemperate use of ardent spirits.

M. & D.

IN GOUT.

Wine of Colchicum Seed....................Three Drams.
Fluid Extract of Opium....................Half Dram.

Dose—Twenty to thirty drops. *Eisenmann.*

JAMES' DIURETIC WINE.

Infusion of Horse Radish....................Six Ounces.
Fluid Extract of Canella....................Three Drams.
" " " Senoka....................Three Drams.
Sherry Wine....................One-and-a-half Pints.

Dose—Two ounces, twice a day.

IN DROPSY AND CHRONIC RHEUMATISM.

Lignum Guaiac. Off....................One Ounce.
Fluid Ext. Black Hellebore....................One "
" " Orange Peel....................Half "
Essence of Cardamon.................... Half "
Wine....................Two Pints.

Dose—Two to three drams, twice a day. *M. & D.*

BITTER WINE IN SCROFULA.

Fluid Extr. Chamomile....................Half Ounce.
" " Cinchona....................Half Ounce.
" " Ginger....................Two Drams.
Carbonate of Potassa....................Three Drams.
Wine....................One-and-a-half Pints.

Dose—Half to one ounce, three times a day. *M. & D.*

RICHARD'S SQUILL WINE.

Fluid Ext. Squill....................One Ounce.
" " Orange Peel....................Two Drams.
" " Blue Flag....................Two Drams.
Oxymel of Squill....................Two Ounces.
Wine....................One Pint.

Dose—Half ounce, four times a day. In dropsy. *M. & D.*

GARGLE TO CORRECT OFFENSIVE BREATH.

Infusion of Cinchona....................Five Ounces.
Chloride of Soda....................One-and-a-half Ounces.
Honey of Roses....................One-and-a-half "
Spirit of Cloves, triturated with a little sugar..Four Drops.

Mix, for a gargle. Used in scurvy, fœtor of the breath, softening of the gums, &c.

HEY'S SCROFULOUS LOTION.

Sulphate of Zinc............................Half Dram.
Spirit of Rosemary..........................One Ounce.
Tincture of Lavender Compound...............One Dram.
Water.......................................Fifteen Ounces.

Mix.

GARGLE AND MOUTH WASH.

Borate of Soda..............................One Ounce.
Rose Water..................................Two Ounces.
Honey.......................................One Ounce.

Mix, and add,

Tincture of Myrrh...........................Half Ounce.
" " Capsicum................................Two Ounces.

Use as a gargle, every two or three hours, diluted with water. *P.*

DENTIFRICES.

1.

Red Bole....................................Three Ounces.
Coral.......................................Three "
Sepia Bone..................................Three "
Dragon's Blood..............................One-and-a-half Ounces.
Cochineal...................................Three Drams.
Cream of Tartar.............................Four-and-a-half Ounces.
Cinnamon....................................Six Drams.
Cloves......................................One Dram.

All to be finely powdered and mixed.

2.

Aromatic Calamus............................Four Drams.
Charcoal....................................One Dram.
Soap..One Dram.
Oil of Cloves...............................Twelve Minims.

3.

Venetian Talc...............................Four Ounces.
Bicarbonate of Soda.........................One Ounce.
Carmine.....................................Five Grains.
Oil of Mint.................................Ten Minims.

4.

Charcoal....................................Four Parts.
Cinchona....................................Two Parts.
Myrrh.......................................One "

5.

Cinchona..Two Ounces.
Orris Powder....................................One Ounce.
Muriate of Ammonia..............................Half Ounce.
Catechu...Six Drams.
Myrrh...Six Drams.
Oil of Cloves...................................Seven Minims.

6.

Camphor (finely pulverized)..................One Part.
Prepared Chalk...............................Three to Seven Parts

---

ANTIARTHRITIC POULTICE.

Bread Crumbs..................................Thirty-two Ounces.
Water...
Alcohol, of each, equal parts.................. Sufficient.

To give the bread crumbs the consistence of a poultice, heat it upon a gentle fire. The poultice being made, add to the surface:

Solid Extract of Opium......................Seventy-five Grains.
" " " Stramonium.................Seventy-five Grains.

Dissolve them in water, and make them of a fluid consistence. Then sprinkle the surface with

Camphor (in powder).........................Half Ounce.

Apply the poultice, when tepid, to the painful joint, and leave it on at least three days. Cover it with oil-cloth or flannel, to keep in the moisture.

T. & R.

SEDATIVE LINIMENT, FOR ULCERATED PILES.

Solid Extract of Stramonium..............Half Dram.
Hydrochlorate of Morphia.................Four-and-a-half Grains.
Yolk of One Egg.

Beat the substances together, to make a liniment. Let fledgets of tow be soaked in it, and applied to the principal hæmorrhoidal tumors.

T. & R.

INDEX TO DISEASES.

Diseases mentioned in the preceding pages, referred to their specific Formulæ.

GENERAL INDEX.

12

T.

U.

V.

X.

Y.

Z.

Finis.

APPENDIX.

Containing formulæ which have appeared in the Journal of Materia Medica, and were not published in the previous editions of the Book of Formulæ.

APPENDIX.

ACHILLEA MILLEFOLIUM.

Yarrow.

Indigenous to Europe and United States. Possesses a faint, pleasant, peculiar fragrance, with a bitterish, astringent, pungent taste, which properties are due to tannic achilleic acids, essential oils, and bitter extractive.

MEDICAL PROPERTIES.

Mild, aromatic tonic, antispasmodic and astringent. Employed in intermittents, flatulent colic and nervous affections, in suppression of hemorrhages, and of profuse mucous discharges, in low forms of exanthematous fevers with difficult eruptions.

PREPARATION.

Fluid Extract.................................Dose. ½ to 1 Dram.

TINCTURE OF YARROW.

Fluid Extract.................................Three Ounces.
Diluted Alcohol...............................Thirteen "
Dose—One-fourth to one-half ounce.

SYRUP OF YARROW.

Fluid Extract.................................Two Ounces.
Diluted Alcohol...............................Fourteen Ounces.
Dose—One-fourth to one ounce.

ANGELICA ATROPURPUREA.

Angelica Root.

A perennial plant, grows in fields and damp places, and flowers from May to August; has a powerful, peculiar, and not disagreeable odor, and sweet taste, somewhat pungent and spicy.

MEDICAL PROPERTIES.

Aromatic, stimulant, carminative, diaphoretic, diuretic, and emmenagogue. Used in flatulent colic, heart-burn, in diseases of the urinary organs, calculi, and passive dropsy as a diuretic, with uva ursi and eupatoreum purpureum.

PREPARATION.

Fluid Extract....................................Dose, ½ to 1 Dram.

TINCTURE OF ANGELICA.

Fluid Extract....................................Two Ounces.
Diluted Alcohol....................................Fourteen Ounces.
Dose—One-fourth to one ounce.

COMPOUND TINCTURE OF ANGELICA.

Fluid Extract....................................One Ounce.
Oil of Anise Seed....................................One-fourth Ounce.
Diluted Alcohol....................................One Pint.
Employed as stomachic and carminative.
Dose—One-half to two fluid drams.

ARALIA HISPIDA.

Dwarf Elder.

A perennial plant, flowering from June to September. The root is the part generally employed in medicine.

MEDICAL PROPERTIES.

Sudorific, diuretic, and alterative. Very valuable in dropsy, gravel, suppression of urine, and urinary disorders generally.

PREPARATION.

Fluid Extract....................................Dose, 1 to 2 Drams.

SYRUP OF DWARF ELDER.

Fluid Extract....................................Six Ounces.
Syrup....................................Ten "
Dose—One-fourth to one ounce.

ARALIA RACEMOSA.

Spikenard.

An indigenous plant, growing in rich woodlands. The root is the medicinal part.

MEDICAL PROPERTIES.

The root is spicy, aromatic, alterative, and gently stimulant. It is much used in pulmonary affections.

PREPARATION.

Fluid Extract.................................Dose, 1 to 3 Drams.

INFUSION OF SPIKENARD.

Fluid Extract.................................Three Ounces.
Water...Nine "
Dose—Half to one and a half ounces.

SYRUP OF SPIKENARD.

Fluid Extract.................................Six Ounces.
Syrup...Ten "
Dose—One-third to one ounce.

ARTEMESIA ABROTANUM.

Southernwood.

A perennial plant; native of the South of Europe; cultivated generally in the gardens; has a fragrant odor, and a warm, bitter, nauseous taste.

MEDICAL PROPERTIES.

Tonic, antispasmodic, and employed in intermittents, to promote the appetite, in atonic dyspepsia, and in debilitated condition of the digestive organs.

PREPARATION.

Fluid Extract.................................Dose, 30 to 60 Drops.

SYRUP OF SOUTHERNWOOD.

Fluid Extract.................................Four Ounces.
Syrup...Twelve "
Dose—One to two drams.

ARTEMESIA VULGARIS.

Mugwort.

A perennial plant; native of Europe; cultivated in this country; the tops and leaves are employed in medicine.

MEDICAL PROPERTIES.

Anthelmintic, tonic and deobstruent; is reputed beneficial in epilepsy, hysteria, and amenorrhœa; employed often as an emmenagogue, and in intermittent fevers; externally used in fomentations for bruises and local inflammations.

PREPARATION.

Fluid Extract.................................Dose, 20 to 40 Drops.

TINCTURE OF MUGWORT.

Fluid Extract.................................Three Ounces.
Diluted Alcohol.................................Thirteen "
Dose—Half to two drams. Used externally.

ARUM TRYPHYLLUM.

Wild Turnip.

The plant is indigenous to the American Continent, in both hemispheres; is found in wet locations, and flowers from May to July. The whole plant is acrid, the root being the officinal part; when fresh, it is very acrid, and causes a persistent and intensely acrid impression on the tongue, lips and fauces. The active principle is rapidly deteriorated by heat.

MEDICAL PROPERTIES.

Acrid, expectorant, diaphoretic; used in flatulence, croup, whooping cough, stomatitis, asthma, chronic laryngitis, bronchitis, low stage of typhus fever, and various affections connected with a cachectic state of the system; externally it has been used with marked success in scrofulous tumors, tinea capitis, and other cutaneous affections.

PREPARATION.

Fluid Extract.................................Dose, 10 to 20 Drops.

TINCTURE OF WILD TURNIP.

Fluid Extract.................................Two Ounces.
Diluted Alcohol.................................Fourteen Ounces.
Dose—One-half to one dram.

SYRUP OF WILD TURNIP.

Fluid Extract.................................Two Ounces.
Syrup.................................Fourteen Ounces.
Dose—One-half to one dram.

BENZOIN ODORIFERUM.

Fever Bush.

Is the *Laurus Benzoin* of Linnæus; grows in damp woods and shady places in the United States and Canadas. The whole plant possesses an aromatic, pleasant taste, due to a volatile oil.

MEDICAL PROPERTIES.

Aromatic, stimulant, and tonic. Used in ague and typhoid forms of fevers, as a refrigerant and exhilarant in various forms of fever, for allaying excessive heat and uneasiness.

PREPARATION.

Fluid Extract.................................Dose, ½ to 1 Dram.

SYRUP OF FEVER BUSH.

Fluid Extract.................................Two Ounces.
Syrup.................................Fourteen Ounces.
Dose—Half to one ounce.

BERBERIS VULGARIS.

Barberry.

Indigenous to the New England, Middle, and Southern States; flowers in April and May, and ripens its fruit in June. Berberina is the active alkaline principle.

MEDICAL PROPERTIES.

Tonic and laxative. Used in cases where tonics are indicated, in jaundice and chronic diarrhœa and dysentery, cholera infantum, etc. Serviceable as a wash or gargle in apthous sore mouth, and in chronic opthalmia.

PREPARATION.

Fluid Extract.................................Dose, ½ to 1 Dram.

SYRUP OF BARBERRY.

Fluid Extract.................................Two Ounces.
Syrup...Fourteen Ounces.
Dose—One-fourth to one ounce.

CHENOPODIUM ANTHELMINTICUM.

Wormseed.

An indigenous perennial plant, growing in almost all parts of the United States, but most vigorously and abundantly in the Southern section. All parts of the plant are occasionally employed; but the globular, unexpanded flowers, commonly called seeds, only are strictly officinal.

MEDICAL PROPERTIES.

Wormseed is one of our most efficient anthelmintics, and is thought to be particularly adapted to the expulsion of the round worms in children. A dose of it usually given before breakfast in the morning, and at bedtime in the evening, for three or four days successively, and then followed by some brisk cathartic.

PREPARATION.

Fluid Extract.................................Dose, 1 to 2 Drams.

INFUSION OF WORMSEED.

Fluid Extract of Wormseed.......................One Ounce.
" " " Orange Peel.......................Two Drams.
Water...Eight Ounces.
Dose—One to two ounces.

SYRUP OF WORMSEED.

Fluid Extract.................................Two Ounces.
Syrup...Six "
Dose—Half to one ounce.

COMPTONIA ASPLENIFOLIA.

Sweet Fern.

A shrubby, indigenous plant, found in the Northern and Middle States, growing in thin, sandy soils, or dry, rocky woods. The entire plant possesses a spicy, aromatic odor, when bruised, and an aromatic, astringent, bitterish taste.

MEDICAL PROPERTIES.

Tonic, astringent, and alterative. Used in diarrhœa, dysentery, hæmoptysis, leucorrhœa, debility succeeding fevers, and in rachitis; is a valuable auxiliary in the summer-complaint of children.

PREPARATION.

Fluid Extract.................................Dose, ½ to 1 Dram.

SYRUP OF SWEET FERN.

Fluid Extract.................................Two Ounces.
Syrup.......................................Fourteen Ounces.
Dose—One to two Drams.

CONVALARIA MULTIFLORA.

Solomon's Seal.

These plants grow on the sides of meadows, high banks, woods and mountains, in the Northern and Eastern States and Canada. The root is the part used in the medicine.

MEDICAL PROPERTIES.

Tonic, mucilaginous, and mildly astringent; of much value in leucorrhœa, menorrhagia, female debility, and pectoral affections. An infusion will be found of great efficacy in irritable conditions of the intestines, as well as in chronic inflammations of these parts, especially when attended with burning sensations, pain, etc.

PREPARATION.

Fluid Extract.................................Dose, 2 to 6 Drams.

INFUSION OF SOLOMON'S SEAL.

Fluid Extract.................................Four Ounces.
Water.......................................Twelve "
Dose—One to four ounces.

COPTIS TRIFOLIA.

Gold Thread.

The root of *Coptis Trifolia*, a small evergreen plant, found in the more Northern parts of both Continents, in wet and boggy situations.

MEDICAL PROPERTIES.

Bitter tonic. Used in cases where a pure bitter tonic is required; and much used as a gargle in various ulcerations of the mouth.

PREPARATION.

Fluid Extract.................................Dose, ½ to 1 Dram.

CUCUMIS COLOCYNTHIS.

Colocynth.

The dried pulp of the fruit of *Citrullus Colocynthis.*

MEDICAL PROPERTIES.

Colocynth is a powerful drastic hydragogue cathartic; seldom prescribed alone; usually given in combination with other cathartics. To allow an easy combination with many fluid extracts, this preparation is offered, of the strength of one ounce of colocynth pulp to one fluid ounce of extract.

PREPARATION.

Fluid Extract................ ....Dose, 5 to 13 Drops.

TINCTURE OF COLOCYNTH.

Fluid Extract.................................Two Ounces.
Oil Anise.................................One-fourth Ounce.
Diluted Alcohol.................................Fourteen Ounces.
Dose—Fifteen to sixty drops.

DIOSCOREA VILLOSA.

Wild Yam.

This is a slender vine, indigenous to the United States and Canada, being rare in the New England States, and more common in the Middle and Southern States. It is sometimes called *Colic Root.* It flowers in June and July.

MEDICAL PROPERTIES.

Antispasmodic. In bilious colic it has considerable reputation—by some considered a specific; in cramp of the stomach or painful spasmodic affections of the bowels; in flatulence and borborygmi, and in nausea and vomiting, of pregnant women, it is particularly recommended.

PREPARATIONS.

Fluid Extract....................................Dose, 5 to 30 Drops.
Dioscorein ...." 1 to 4 Grains.

Fluid Extract of Wild Yam, } ....Equal Parts.
" " Cornin, }

Dose—Ten to sixty drops. Used in nausea, and vomiting of pregnant women.

Fluid Extract of Ginger, } ....Equal Parts.
" " Wild Yam, }

Dose—Ten to sixty drops. Useful in flatulence, etc.

ERECTHRITES HIERACIFOLIUS.

Fire Weed.

Is an indigenous plant, growing rank in recent clearings, and particularly in those that have been burned over. It flowers from June to July.

MEDICAL PROPERTIES.

Tonic, astringent, and alterative. Has reputation in diseases of the mucous tissues of the lungs, stomach and bowels, in the treatment of cholera and dysentery, and in the summer-complaints of children.

PREPARATION.

Fluid Extract....................................Dose, ½ to 1 Dram.

EUPATORIUM PURPUREUM.

Queen of the Meadow.

Grows in low places, flowering in August and September. The root is the part employed in medicine.

MEDICAL PROPERTIES.

Employed as a diuretic in dropsical affections. Is recommended in strangury, gravel, and all chronic urinary disorders, hæmaturia, gout and rheumatism.

PREPARATION.

Fluid Extract.................................Dose, 1 to 3 Drams.
Eupurpurin.................................. " 3 to 4 Grains.

SYRUP OF QUEEN OF THE MEADOW.

Fluid Extract.................................Four Ounces.
Syrup...Ten "
Dose—Three to six drams.

GALIUM APERINE.

Cleavers.

Common in Europe and the United States, growing in moist places, along banks of rivers and streams. Flowers from June to September.

MEDICAL PROPERTIES.

Valuable as a refrigerant and diuretic, and beneficial in many diseases of the urinary organs, as suppression of urine, calculous affections, inflammation of the kidneys and bladder, and in the scalding of the urine in gonorrhœa. It is contra-indicated in diseases of a passive character, on account of its refrigerant and sedative effects upon the system, but may be used freely in fevers and all acute diseases.

PREPARATION.

Fluid Extract.................................Dose, 1 to 2 Drams.

GEUM RIVALE.

Avens Root.

Indigenous to the United States, grows in moist meadows and localities. Flowers from June to August. The green plant possesses medicinal properties; the root is the officinal part.

MEDICAL PROPERTIES.

Tonic and astringent. Used in numerous diseases, as chronic hemorrhages, chronic diarrhœa and dysentery, leucorrhœa, dyspepsia, phthisis, congestions of the abdominal viscera, intermittents, ulcerations, etc.

PREPARATION.

Fluid Extract.................................Dose, ½ to 1 Dram.

HELIANTHEUM CANADENSE.

Frostwort.

It grows throughout the United States, in dry, sandy soils; flowers from May to July. The entire plant is officinal. Sometimes called *Rock Rose.*

MEDICAL PROPERTIES.

Tonic, astringent, and alterative. Held as valuable in scrofula, secondary syphilis and cutaneous diseases, as a gargle in scarlatina, and apthous ulcerations.

PREPARATION.

Fluid Extract..................................Dose, 1 to 2 Drams.

SYRUP OF FROSTWORT.

Fluid Extract..................................Two Ounces.
Syrup..Fourteen Ounces.
Dose—Two to eight drams.

HYPERICUM PERFORATUM.

Johnswort.

Indigenous to Europe and the United States, growing upon dry localities; flowers from June to August. It possesses a peculiar odor, and a balsamic, bitterish, astringent taste.

MEDICAL PROPERTIES.

Astringent, sedative, and diuretic. Used in chronic urinary affections, suppression of the urine, diarrhœa, dysentery, nervous affections, hæmoptysis, and other affections.

PREPARATION.

Fluid Extract..................................Dose, ½ to 1 Dram.

INULA HELONIUM.

Elecampane.

The Elecampane is common in Europe and in this country, growing along the road-sides, in pastures, and rich places; flowers from July to September. The root is the officinal part. Should not be used medicinally until the seconed year of growth, and should then be collected in the fall.

MEDICAL PROPERTIES.

An aromatic stimulant and tonic, expectorant, diuretic, and diaphoretic. Used in chronic pulmonary affections, weakness of the digestive organs, dyspepsia, and cutaneous diseases.

PREPARATION.

Fluid Extract.................................Dose, ½ to 1 Dram.

SYRUP OF ELECAMPANE.

Fluid Extract....................................Four Ounces.
Syrup....... ....Twelve "
Dose—One to two Drams.

COMPOUND SYRUP OF ELECAMPANE.

Fluid Extract Elecampane..................Two Ounces.
" " Foxglove....................Three Drams.
" " Ipecac....................... " "
" " Opium.......................One and one-half Drams.
Syrup ....Thirtee Ounces.
Dose—One-half to one dram, four to six times a day, in chronic catarrh.

JUNIPERUS COMMUNIS.

Juniper.

Native of Europe, though naturalized in some parts of this country, growing in dry woods and hills, and flowering in May. The berries are officinal.

MEDICAL PROPERTIES.

Juniper berries are gently stimulant and diuretic. Used cheifly as an adjuvant to more powerful diuretics in dropsical complaints; but have been recommended also in scorbutic and cutaneous diseases, catarrh of the bladder, and atonic conditions of the alimentary canal and uterus.

PREPARATION.

Fluid Extract....................................Dose, 1 to 2 Drams.

INFUSION OF JUNIPER.

Fluid Extract....................................One Ounce.
Water ....Half Pint.
Dose—One to three ounces.

COMPOUND DECOCTION OF BROOM.

Fluid Extract of Broom.................................Half Ounce.
" " Juniper...................... .... " "
" " Dandelion........................... " "
Water.................................. ....One Pint.
Dose—Three to six ounces.

LIGUSTICUM LEVISTICUM.

Lovage.

Found growing wild in the South of Europe, and cultivated in gardens; upon that Continent, chiefly found in gardens. The root, stem, leaves and seeds have all been employed in medicine. The seeds and root are the most esteemed.

MEDICAL PROPERTIES.

Stimulant aromatic. Used as a carminative and diaphoretic; often added to purgative preparations, on account of its aromatic carminative properties.

PREPARATION.

Fluid Extract..................... ....Dose, ½ to 1 Dram.

LIRIODENDRON TULIPIFERA.

White Wood.

This is one of the most magnificent trees of the American forests, on account of its elegant appearance, its therapeutical virtues, and the value of its wood. The part employed in medicine is the bark of both trunk and root.

MEDICAL PROPERTIES.

Aromatic, stimulant, and tonic. Used in intermittents, chronic rheumatism, chronic, gastric and intestinal diseases, hectic fever, night sweats, and colliquative diarrhœa of phthisis.

PREPARATION.

Fluid Extract....................................Dose, ½ to 2 Drams.

MYRICA GALE.

Sweet Gale.

Found in dry woods, or in open pastures, from Canada to Florida.

MEDICAL PROPERTIES.

Used as an astringent in diarrhœa, dysentery, and diseases where astringent stimulants are indicated.

PREPARATIONS.

Fluid Extract.......................................Dose, ½ to 1 Dram.

NYMPHEA ODORATA.

White Lily.

This plant is found in ponds, marshes, etc., in most parts of the United States. It flowers from June to September; the flowers close at night and open about sunrise; and the seeds ripen under water.

MEDICAL PROPERTIES.

Astringent, demulcent, anodyne and alterative. Used in dysentery, diarrhœa, leucorrhœa, scrofula, and combined with wild cherry in bronchial affections.

PREPARATION.

Fluid Extract.......................................Dose, ½ to 1 Dram.

SYRUP OF WHITE POND LILY.

Fluid Extract.......................................Two Ounces.
Syrup.......................................Fourteen "
Dose—One to four Drams.

POPULUS TREMULOIDES.

Poplar.

This tree is common in Lower Canada and in the Northern and Middle States. The bark is officinal, and should be collected early in the Spring.

MEDICAL PROPERTIES.

Tonic and febrifuge. Used in intermittents, debility, impared digestion, chronic diarrhœa, etc.

PREPARATION.

Fluid Extract.................................Dose, ½ to 1 Dram.

PTELEA TRIFOLIATA.

Wafer Ash.

Is a shrub common to this country, growing abundantly West of the Alleghanies, in shady, moist hedges and in rocky places; flowers in June. The bark is officinal.

MEDICAL PROPERTIES.

Is a tonic. Used in intermittent fevers, remittent fevers, and all cases where tonics are indicated. Is recommended in asthma and pulmonary affections, and is stated to be tolerated by the stomach when other tonics are rejected.

PREPARATIONS.

Fluid Extract.................................Dose 15 to 60 Drops.
Ptelein.................................. "

TINCTURE PTELEA.

Fluid Extract.....................................Four Ounces.
Diluted Alcohol.................................Twelve "

Dose—One to two Drams.

COMPOUNDS OF PTELEA.

I.

Ptelein, Xanthoxylin equal parts, given in dyspepsia, in doses of one or two grains, two or three times a day. If constipation be present, use the following:

II.

Ptelein.......................................Nineteen Grains.
Alcoholic Extract Nux Vomica ....One Grain.
Sugar, or Sugar of Milk.......................Two Drams.

Dose—Six grains three or four times a day.

III.

Podophyllin...One Grain.
Leptandrin.. " "
Sulphate Quinia...................................Four Grains.
Ptelein...Eight "

Divide into eight pills.

Dose—One pill two or three times a day in chronic erysipelas, habitual constipation and some forms of dyspepsia.

PULMONARIA OFFICINALIS.

Lungwort.

The plant is found in alluvial banks, from Western New York to Georgia, and the Western States. The leaves are the part used in medicine.

MEDICAL PROPERTIES.

Demulcent and mucilaginous. Used in hemorrhage from the lungs, in bronchial and catarrhal affections, and in pulmonary affections generally.

PREPARATION.

Fluid Extract....................................Dose, ½ to 1 Dram.

PYRETHRUM PARTHENIUM.

Fever Few.

Is an European plant, cultivated in the United States generally; seldom found in wild state. Flowers in June and July.

MEDICAL PROPERTIES.

Tonic, stimulant, carminative, emmenagogue, and vermifuge. Used in flatulency, hysteria, worms, irregular menstruation, suppression of the urine, and in some febrile diseases.

PREPARATION.

Fluid Extract....................................Dose, ½ to 1 Dram.

SABBATIA ANGULARIS.

Red Centaury.

This plant is common in most parts of the United States, growing in moist meadows, in damp rich soils. Flowers from June to September.

MEDICAL PROPERTIES.

Employed as a tonic in full periodic febrile diseases, both as a preventive and as a remedy, as a bitter tonic, in dyspepsia and convalescence from fevers.

PREPARATION.

Fluid Extract....................................Dose, ½ to 1 Dram.

SAMBUCUS CANADENSIS.

Elder Flowers.

Indigenous to all parts of the United States. Flowers in June and July. The officinal parts are the flowers, berries and the inner bark.

MEDICAL PROPERTIES.

Diaphoretic, diuretic, alterative, and gently stimulating. Used in measles, erysipelas, and erysipelatous diseases, etc.

PREPARATION.

Fluid Extract....................................Dose, ½ to 1 Dram.

SYRUP OF ELDER FLOWERS.

Fluid Extract....................................Four Ounces.
Syrup....................................Twelve "
Dose—One to two drams.

COMPOUND SYRUP OF ELDER FLOWERS.

Fluid Extract Elder Flowers		Eight Ounces.
" "	Prickly Ash	" "
" "	Blue Flag	" "
" "	Sassafras	" "
" "	Yellow Dock	Ten "
" "	Burdock	" "
" "	Sarsap. (Amer.)	" "
Syrup		Twelve Pints.

Dose—One to two drams two or three times a day.

SOLIDAGO ODORA.

Golden Rod.

This plant is common in most parts of the United States. growing along the fences of pastures. There are several varieties, which differ from each other in their degree of astringency and fragrance. The Solidago Odora is the variety highest in repute in medicine.

MEDICAL PROPERTIES.

Diaphoretic, carminative and stimulant. Used in flatulent colic, in convalescence from severe dysentery, diarrhœa, cholera morbus, etc.

PREPARATION.

Fluid Extract..................................Dose, ½ to 1 Dram.

STATICE CAROLINIANA.

Marsh Rosemary.

Marsh Rosemary, is common to the salt-marshes, or Atlantic shores of the United States. Flowers from August to October. The root is the officinal part, and contains a large percentage of tannic acid.

MEDICAL PROPERTIES.

Powerful astringent, with sudorific properties. Used in the treatment of diarrhœa, apthous and ulcerative affections of the mouth and fauces, as a gargle in putrid sore throat, and in dysentery after the acute stage is passed. Applied externally, it is valuable in piles; and as an injection, in chronic gonorrhœa, gleet, leucorrhœa, etc.

PREPARATION.

Fluid Extract..................................Dose, 15 to 40 Drops.

SYRUP OF MARSH ROSEMARY.

Fluid Extract..................................Four Ounces.
Syrup..................................Twelve "
Dose—One-half to one teaspoonful.

SYMPHYTUM OFFICINALE.

Comfrey.

A perennial European plant, much cultivated in our gardens for medicinal purposes. The root is the officinal part.

MEDICAL PROPERTIES.

The therapeutic effects of the comfrey are due to its mucilaginous properties, which act upon the mucous membranes. It is demulcent and somewhat astringent. Useful in diarrhœa, dysentery, coughs, hæmoptysis, other pulmonary affections, leucorrhœa and female debility.

PREPARATION.

Fluid Extract..................................Dose, 2 to 4 Drams.

INFUSION OF COMFREY.

Fluid Extract	Six Ounces.
Water	Ten "

Dose—Half to two ounces.

SYRUP OF COMFREY.

Fluid Extract	Four Ounces.
Syrup	Six "

Dose—Two to six drams.

PULMONARY BALSAM.

Fluid Extract of Comfrey	One Dram.
" " Spikenard	" "
" " Elecampane	" "
" " Bloodroot	" "
" " Horehound	" "
" " Wild Cherry	" "
Alcohol	Ten "
Syrup	Eight Ounces.

Dose—Half to one ounce.

TANACETUM VULGARE.

Double Tansey.

Tansey is cultivated in gardens, and in some localities is found growing wild in the roads and old fields. Flowers from July to September.

MEDICAL PROPERTIES.

Tonic, diaphoretic, and emmenagogue. Used as an aromatic bitter in intermittents, hysteria, amenorrhœa, and as an anthelmintic.

PREPARATION.

Fluid Extract....Dose, ½ to 1 Dram.

COMPOUND SYRUP OF TANSEY.

Fluid Extract Tansey	One Ounce.
" " Wormwood	Three Ounces.
" " Rhei	" "
Sherry Wine	Two "
Syrup	Twenty "

Dose—One to two fluid drams, two or three times a day, as a vermifuge.

THYMUS VULGARIS.

Thyme.

Is indigenous to the South of Europe, and with us is cultivated in gardens.

MEDICAL PROPERTIES.

Tonic, carminative, emmenagogue, and antispasmodic. Used as a stimulating tonic in hysteria, dysmenorrhœa, flatulence, colic, headache, etc.

PREPARATION.

Fluid Extract.................................Dose, ½ to 1 Dram.

TUSSILAGO FARFARA.

Coltsfoot.

Indigenous to Europe and America. Grows in wet places, and upon the sides of small streams. The leaves and roots are both used in medicine.

MEDICAL PROPERTIES.

Emollient, demulcent and tonic. Employed in coughs, asthma, whooping cough, and pulmonary diseases.

PREPARATION.

Fluid Extract.................................Dose, ½ to 1 Dram.

VERBENA.

Vervain.

Indigenous to the United States. The root and tops are used in medicine.

MEDICAL PROPERTIES.

Tonic, emetic, expectorant, and sudorific. Used in intermittent fever, obstructed menstruation, in scrofula, and visceral obstructions.

PREPARATION.

Fluid Extract.................................Dose, ½ to 1 Dram.

VIBURNUM OPULUS.

Cramp Bark, or High Cranberry.

Is a handsome indigenous shrub, growing in low, rich lands, in the northern part of the United States and Canada; flowering in June.

MEDICAL PROPERTIES.

Is a powerful antispasmodic, and in consequence of this property received the name of *Cramp Bark.* Is used in asthma, spasms, cramps, and for females subject to convulsions during pregnancy, or at the time of parturition; it is said to prevent these attacks entirely, if used daily for the last two or three months of gestation.

PREPARATIONS.

Fluid Extract.................................Dose, 1 to 2 Drams.
Vibernin.................................... "

COMPOUND TINCTURE OF CRAMP BARK.

Fluid Extract	Cramp Bark	....	Two Ounces
" "	Lobelia	....	One Ounce.
" "	Skunk Cabbage	....	" "
" "	Stramonium	....	Half "
" "	Capsicum	....	" "
" "	Bloodroot	....	" "
Alcohol		....	Three and one-half Pints.

Dose—Twenty to sixty drops, in asthma, hysteria, and all nervous disorders.

Miscellaneous Formulæ.

DENTAL ANÆSTHETIC.

By Dr. Tefft.

Tincture of Aconite..............................	One Ounce.
Chloroform..............................	" "
Alcohol..............................	" "
Morphine..............................	Six Grains.

Mix. To prevent the pain of extraction, and destroy sensibility in the gums by local application. Moisten two fledges of cotton with the liquid, and apply to the gums for a minute or two over the tooth to be extracted.

IN FEVER AND AGUE.

Furnished by P. Barnes.

Yellow Bark................................Four Ounces.
Cream of Tartar............................Half Ounce.
Cloves.....................................Thirty.
Sherry Wine................................One Quart.

Digest for twenty-four hours.

Dose—A wine-glass full at the first indication of the fit, another in thirty minutes, and a third thirty minutes after the second.

COUGH MIXTURE.

Furnished by P. Barnes.

Elixir Paregoric...........................One Ounce.
Emetic Tartar..............................Eight Grains.
Syrup Squill...............................Half Ounce.
Gum Arabic.................................. " "
Spiritus Mindereri......................... " Pint.

Dose—Mix one dram in sweetened water; take sufficient to produce a slight nausea.

IN DROPSICAL AFFECTIONS.

Furnished by V. C. Howe, M. D.

Podophyllin................................Four Grains.
Bitartrate of Potassa......................Three Drams.

Mix, and divide into eight powders.

Dose—One every two hours.

IN ACNE SIMPLEX.

By B. C. Stiles.

Hyd. Chl. Corrosiv.........................Five Grains.
Aqua Rosæ..................................One Ounce.

Mix. Apply to the affected part.

NEW HÆMOSTATIC.

By M. Larin.

Decoction of Rhatany.......................Thirty Parts.
Alum.......................................Six Parts.

If given internally, seven parts of syrup are to be added. Internally, ten drams may be given three times, daily; while for external use, it may be employed as an injection or lotion.

ANODYNE LOTION.

Prussic Acid...............................One Dram.
Glycerine.................................. " "
Aconitina.................................. " Grain.

Apply with a camel's hair pencil over parts affected with severe neuralgic pains.

HOPE'S MIXTURE FOR DYSENTERY.

Nitric Acid.. ....Eight Drops.
Tincture of Opium..............................Forty "
Camphor Water..................................Eight Ounces.
Mix. Dose—A tablespoonful.

BELL'S GARGLE.

Borate of Soda........................ ....Two Drams.
Yeast..Half Ounce.
Honey... " "
Boiling Water...................................Seven Ounces.
Mix.

EYE WATER.

Borate of Soda..................................Half Dram.
Camphor Water............................ ....Three Ounces.
M. Cola. Excellent in acute opthalmia.

A MILD AND EFFICIENT CATHARTIC.

Furnished by J. F. Morey, Vandalia, Ill.

Gum Gamboge....................................Half Part.
Jalap...One "
Socotrine Aloes................................ " "
Rhubarb .... " "
Extract of Boneset.............................Sufficient.

From the Philadelphia Medical and Surgical Journal.

IN WHOOPING-COUGH.

I.

Iodide of Silver ....Thirty Grains.
Syrup of Ipecac.................................One Ounce.
" " Wild Cherry..........................Four Ounces.

II.

Iodide of Silver ....Thirty Grains.
Tincture of Aconite Root.......................One Drop.
Syrup of Ipecac................................ " Dram.
" " Garlic............................... " "
Mucilage of Gum Arabic.......................Two Ounces.
M. Dose—A teaspoonful.

Furnished by A. King, M. D.

Dried Capsules of the Æsculus Hippocastanum
(bruised coarsely)..............................One Ounce.
Good Rye Whiskey (half water)..................One Quart.
Dose—One dram. With Cimicifuga and Ergot for consumption and as a parturient.

IN GONORRHEA.

Furnished by J. J. Irby, M. D.

Bal. Copaiba....................................Five Drams
White Sugar....................................Two "
Yellow of an Egg..............................
Water...Eight Ounces.

Inject with this three or four times a day. It is preferable to anything I have ever used.

RHEUMATISM.

By Dr. Horton.

Tincture of Strychnos ....One Ounce.
" " Cimicifuga.............................Two Ounces.
Muriate of Morphine ....Twelve Grains.

Dose—Thirty to sixty drops, four times per day.

IN FACIAL AND DENTAL NEURALGIA.

Furnished by W. Davidson, M. D., Charleston, Iowa.

Solid Extract of Belladonna ....Four Grains.
Aqua Ammonia.................................Six Drams.
Spts. Turpentine...............................Half Ounce.
Tinct. Opium...................................Two Drams.
Olive Oil..Half Ounce.

Mix. Apply during the paroxysm.

IN DISMENORRHŒA.

Furnished by W. Pope, M. D., Hinckly, Ohio.

Tinct. Gelseminum...............................One Ounce.
" Cypripedium...................... ....Three Ounces.
" Caulophyllum..............................Two "
" Camphor.....................................One Ounce.

LIQUOR ERGOTÆ.

Secale Cornet. Contus..........................Three Pounds.
Aqua...Eight Pints.

Macerate for twelve hours, and add

Spirit Rectif...................................Four "

Digest for fourteen days and filter.

Dose—A teaspoonful.

Eight times stronger than the infusion; two-and-a-half times stronger than the tincture of the Apothecaries Hall.

The above is an old English Formulæ, sent to us by a distinguished pharmaceutist in Washington. The Liquor prepared in this way is in general use by the profession in that section, and is considered reliable.

HEPHATIC PILLS.

Furnished by W. Pope, M. D.

Podophyllin . . . . .Twenty Grains.
Leptandrin. . . . . .Thirty "
Sanguinarin. . . . . .Twenty "
Hydrastin. . . . . " "
Capsicum. . . . . .Ten Grains.

Make Pills with two parts Extract Taraxaci and one part Extract Hyoscyamus.

COOK'S PILL.

Calomel. . . . . .One Part.
Rhubub. . . . . " "
Aloes. . . . . " "

Mix, and make into four-grain pills. These are in extensive use on the plantations at the South.

TASTELESS FEBRIFUGE POWDER FOR CHILDREN.

Pure Quinia (not sulphate). . . . . .Forty-five Grains.
Sugar. . . . . .Two-and-a-half Drams.

Triturate with care in a porcelain mortar, and divide into eight powders. To be given in a little preserve as follows: One each day for two days, then a day of rest; the following day a packet, then two days of rest; then another packet, and three days rest; and so on. Tannate of Quinia can be substituted for pure Quinia.

IN DISORDERED MENSTRUATION.

Furnished by S. R. Wells, M. D., Waterloo, N. Y.

Iron by Hydrogen. . . . . .One Grain.
Aloes. . . . . .Two-thirds Grain.
Ipecac. . . . . .One-half "
Ignatia Amara. . . . . " "

One of the best female pills known.

LEPTANDRIA CORDIAL.

Furnished by Dr. Davis, Charleston, Ill.

Leptandrin. . . . . .Eight Ounces.
Rhubarb. . . . . .Four "
Bayberry . . . . " "
Ginger. . . . . .Two "
Cloves. . . . . .One "
Peppermint. . . . . .Two "
Myrrh. . . . . " "
Soda, S. C. . . . . " "

Alcohol and water q. s. to obtain the strength.

Dose—One to two teaspoonfuls.

RESTORATIVE WINE BITTERS.

Fluid Extract of Solomon's Seal..................One Ounce.
" " Comfrey........................ " "
" " Spikenard .... " "
" " Chamomile......................Half "
" " Colombo......................... " "
" " Gentian.......................... " "
Sherry Wine....................................Four Pints,

Dose—Half to two ounces.

ANTI-BILIOUS PILL.

Furnished by H. Joslyn, M. D., Syracuse, N. Y.

Aloes...Four Ounces.
Gamboge......................................Two "
Jalap or Colocynth Pulvis......................One Ounce.
Calomel....................................... " "
Castile soap................................... " "
Oil of Anise................................... " Dram.

Pulverize, mix, and wet with water. It acts upon all parts of the intestinal canal, does not nauseate, causes free discharge of the bile, and leaves the bowels in good condition.

NEUTRALIZING CORDIAL.

Furnished by Dr. Davis, Charleston, Ill.

Rhubarb.......................................Eight Ounces.
Saffron..Two "
Cardamon Seeds............................... " "
Nutmegs....................................... " "
Soda, S. C..................................... " "
Essence Peppermint............................ " "
Sugar (refined)................................Two Pounds.

Brandy and water q. s. to obtain the strength.

Dose—One to two teaspoonfuls.

CHERRY CORDIAL.

Furnished by Dr. Davis, Charleston, Ill.

Wild Cherry Bark.............................Sixteen Ounces
Poplar Bark.................................. " "
Sumach....................................... " "
Peach Meats.................................. " "
Brandy (good)................................One Gallon.
Sugar (refined)...............................Eight Pounds.

Dose—One to two teaspoonfuls.

One of the most pleasant and efficient remedies ever got up for bowel complaints, requiring a tonic and astringent remedy.

IN DYSPEPSIA AND CONSTIPATION.

Furnished by Dr. Watson, Utica, N. Y.

Aloes.......................................Two Grains.
Nux Vomica..................................Quarter Grain.

An efficacious and excellent laxative pill.

ANTI-BILIOUS CATHARTIC PILL.

Furnished by Dr. Myers, South Bend, Ind.

Pulv. Rhubub................................Two Scruples.
Podophyllin.................................1½ "
Leptandrin..................................One Scruple.
Extract Nux Vomica..........................Twelve Grains.
Extract Hyosciamus..........................One Dram.
Oil of Anise................................Eight Drops.
Syrup.......................................q. s.

Mix. Make sixty pills.

FEVER AND AGUE PILL.

By Dr. Ware.

Sulphate of Quinine.........................One Grain.
Leptandrin..................................Three Grains.
Podophyllin.................................Quarter Grain.

Dose—One pill two or three times a day.

TONIC.

Furnished by Asa F. Patten, Warner, Merrimac Co., N. H.

Citrate of Iron, sol........................Half Dram.
Sulphate of Iron............................Twenty Grains.
" Quinine...................................Two Scruples.
Simple Syrup................................Four Ounces.
Oil of Sassafras............................Ten Drops.

Mix. Take from one to three teaspoonfuls three or four times a day.

DIARRHŒA PILL.

By Dr. Pratt.

Nit. Argenti................................Quarter Grain.
Sulph. Morphine.............................Eighth "

Pulverize with Gum Arabic.—SMALL PILL.

Dose—One pill two or three times per day.

LEUCORRHŒA.

By Dr. Terrell.

Ferri et Ammoniæ Sulph......................Three Grains.
Fluid Extract Cimicifuga....................Thirty Drops.
" " Colombo.................................. " "
" " Cubebs....................................Fifteen "

ELIXIR CALASAYA BARK.

Take of Calasaya Bark........................Sixteen Ounces.
Orange Peel........................Two "
Cardamon........................Two Drams.
Cinnamon, (Ceylon)........................One Ounce.
Alcohol........................5½ Pints.

Water q. s. to displace six and a half pints tincture, then add three pints of simple syrup and half a pint of rose water.

IMPROVED CATHARTIC PILL.

Comp. Alc. Ext. Colocynth........................One part.
Alc. Ext. Jalap........................One-half part.
Podophyllin........................ " "
Leptandrin........................ " "
Alc. Ext. Hyoscyamus........................One-fourth part.
Ext. Gentian........................One-eighth part.
Oil of Peppermint........................q. s.

Make two-and-a-half grain pills. Dose, one to four.

DR. ATLEE'S NIPPLE WASH.

Furnished by Dr. Edwin A. Atlee.

Pulv. Gum Arabic........................Half Dram.
Biborate of Soda........................Ten Grains.
Tincture of Myrrh........................One Dram.

COMPOUND SYRUP OF MORPHIA.

Jackson's Cough Syrup.

Syrup of Morphia........................Three Ounces.
" Ipecac and Senega........................One Ounce.
" Rhubarb, simple........................ "

Mix.

SIG.—A teaspoonful three times a day.

Receipts for the Syrup of Morphia, Ipecac and Senega used in the above preparation:—

SYRUP OF MORPHIA.

Muriate of Morphia........................One Grain.
Simple Syrup........................One Ounce.
Oil of Sassafras........................Two Drops.

Mix.

SYRUP IPECAC AND SENEGA.

Polygala Senega Root..........................Two Ounces.
Pulverized Ipecac..........................One Dram.
Water..........................Half Gallon.

Boil the Senega Root in the water until half consumed; strain, then add the Ipecac, and sugar enough to form a syrup.

COMPOUND ARNICA LINIMENT.

Huxley's Liniment.

Tincture of Arnica..........................Four-and-a-half Ounces.
Oil of Camphor..........................Half Ounce.
Tincture of Opium..........................One Ounce.

Mix.

BAKER'S COUGH DROPS.

Tincture of Hyoscyamus..........................Four Ounces.
" Digitalis..........................Two "
Syrup of Squill..........................Eight "
Syrup of Balsam of Tolu..........................Two "

Mix.

Dose—One teaspoonful on going to bed.

TO PREVENT THE RECURRENCE OF AGUE.

Furnished by D. L. McGugin, M. D.

Extract Cinchona, (solid)..........................Two Drams.
" Humulus Lup..........................One-and-a-half Drams.
Sulphate Quinine..........................One Scruple.
Extract Rhei..........................One Dram.
Tinct. Zinziber Officinal.......................... "
Aromat. Sulph. Acid..........................Fifty Drops.
Aqua Cinnamomi..........................Six Ounces.

M. ft. mistura.

PIL. COLOCYNTH. MAG.

Presented by A. P. Sharp, of Baltimore.

Ext. Colocynth Comp..........................One Dram.
Hyd. Proto-chlor..........................Twelve Grains.
Tart. Antim. and Pot..........................Two Grains.

Make into twelve pills.

RICHARD'S COUGH MIXTURE.

By Dr. Wolcott Richards.

Tart. Antim................................One Grain.
Pulv. Ext. Glycyrrh........................Two Grains.
Aq. fluvialis..............................One Ounce.
Syr. Scillæ................................ " "
Syr. Tolu.................................. " "
Tinct. Opii. Camph......................... " "
Spt. Nit. dulc.............................Two Drams.

Mix.

RICHARD'S CHALK MIXTURE.

By Dr. Wolcott Richards.

Cretæ Precip...............................One Ounce.
Sacch. Alb................................. " "
Tr. Lavandulæ Comp......................... "
Tr. Kino................................... " "
Ess. Cinnamomi.............................Fifteen Drops.
Aq. font...................................Three Ounces.
Tr. Opii...................................One Dram.

MARSHALL'S PILLS.

By Dr. Vincent C. Marshall.

Comp. Ext. Colocynth.......................One Dram.
Mass. Hydrarg.............................. " "
Pulv. Aloes................................ "
" Sapon Castil............................. "
" Rhei...................................... "

Make into five grain pills.

JUDKINS' PILL.

By Dr. William Judkins.

Mass. Hydr.................................One Dram.
Comp. Ext. Colocynth....................... " "
Ipecac. Pulv...............................One Scruple.
Pulv. Rad. Rhei............................Two Scruples.
Sapon. Castil..............................One Dram.

Mix. and make into five grain pills.

EMBROCATION FOR SPINAL IRRITATION.

By E. M. Hale, M. D., Jonesville, Michigan.

Fluid Extract Aconite......................One Ounce.
" " Arnica..................................Eight Ounces.
Water...................................... " "

Apply with soft flannel to tender and sensitive portions of the spine, twice daily. I have never failed to give relief with this preparation.

BLACK SALVE.

Olive Oil	Twenty Ounces.
Lard	Sixteen "
Mutton Suet	"
Litharge	Fourteen

Melt the oils and fats, and when hot, stir in the litharge (in fine powder), and boil until it becomes of a brown color, then add

Resin	Eight Ounces.
Yellow Wax	" "

Color with a small quantity of Ivory Black, and when nearly cold pour into paper moulds.

ALTERATIVE PILL.

By C. B. Hall, Miller's, Ohio.

Pulv. Sanguinaria Radix	One Ounce.
" Ipecacuanha	Three Drams.
Rhei and Aloes, each	" "
Syrup	q. s.

Make four grain pills.

Dose—One pill three times a day before meals.

This is a most excellent adjuvant in the treatment of atonic dyspepsia; in dry costive habits, with hepatic torpor.

HOOPING-COUGH SYRUP.

By Dr. E. A. Allee.

For a child from six months to

	1 year			Hydrocyanic Acid,	1	Drop;	Simple	Syrup	One Ounce.
From	1	"	to 2	"	"	2	"	"	"	"
"	2		to 4			3			"	
"	4		to 8			4			"	
	8		to 12			6				
"	12		to 15			7	"			
	15	"	to 25		"	8	"	"		"

SIG.—"A teaspoonful two or three times a day. If there is much oppression give a dose of Antimonial Wine before taking the syrup; and if costive, give a dose of Calomel and Rhubarb."

This prescription is so designed that a teaspoonful shall be a dose in each case.

www.ingramcontent.com/pod-product-compliance
Lightning Source LLC
Chambersburg PA
CBHW030325270326
41926CB00010B/1508